TECHNICAL AND ECONOMIC
IMPACT OF CO-GENERATION

Steam Plant Committee

TECHNICAL AND ECONOMIC IMPACT OF CO-GENERATION

Papers presented at a Seminar organized by the Steam
Plant Committee of the Power Industries Division of the
Institution of Mechanical Engineers and held at the
Institution of Mechanical Engineers on
Thursday 22 May 1986

Published by
Mechanical Engineering Publications Limited for
The Institution of Mechanical Engineers
LONDON

First published 1986

ISBN 0 85298 605 X

Printed by Waveney Printed Services Ltd, Beccles, Suffolk

CONTENTS

The Institution of Mechanical Engineers

The primary purpose of the 76,000-member Institution of Mechanical Engineers, formed in 1847, has always been and remains the promotion of standards of excellence in British mechanical engineering and a high level of professional development, competence and conduct among aspiring and practising members. Membership of IMechE is highly regarded by employers, both within the UK and overseas, who recognise that its carefully monitored academic training and responsibility standards are second to none. Indeed they offer incontrovertible evidence of a sound formation and continuing development in career progression.

In pursuit of its aim of attracting suitably qualified youngsters into the profession — in adequate numbers to meet the country's future needs — and of assisting established Chartered Mechanical Engineers to update their knowledge of technological developments — in areas such as CADCAM, robotics and FMS, for example — the IMechE offers a comprehensive range of services and activities. Among these, to name but a few, are symposia, courses, conferences, lectures, competitions, surveys, publications, awards and prizes. A Library containing 150,000 books and periodicals and an Information Service which uses a computer terminal linked to databases in Europe and the USA are among the facilities provided by the Institution.

If you wish to know more about the membership requirements or about the Institution's activities listed above — or have a friend or relative who might be interested — telephone or write to IMechE in the first instance and ask for a copy of our colour 'at a glance' leaflet. This provides fuller details and the contact points — both at the London HQ and IMechE's Bury St Edmunds office — for various aspects of the organisation's operation. Specifically it contains a tear-off slip through which more information on any of the membership grades (Student, Graduate, Associate Member, Member and Fellow) may be obtained.

Corporate members of the Institution are able to use the coveted letters 'CEng, MIMechE' or 'CEng, FIMechE' after their name, designations instantly recognised by, and highly acceptable to, employers in the field of engineering. There is no way other than by membership through which they can be obtained!

The technical and economic aspects of refuse fired CHP plant

M J ROWLEY, BSc, CEng, MIMechE, MBIM
Assistant Chief Design Engineer, Kennedy & Donkin Consulting Engineers

SYNOPSIS A review is made of the technical and economic factors associated with the installation and operation of refuse fired combined heat and power plant. Discussion focusses upon the design and economic aspects of the plant taking into consideration such factors as plant capacity, heat and electricity tariffs, refuse disposal policy, operation and maintenance costs, environmental impact and finally some comparisons with overseas practice.

1   INTRODUCTION AND BACKGROUND

In comparison with many overseas countries the role of combined heat and power (CHP) in the United Kingdom plays only a minor part in meeting industrial and domestic heat and power requirements.

If a further comparison is made of the extent to which refuse incineration is used to provide a source of energy it becomes apparent that UK practice differs considerably.

In both of the above aspects it has to be acknowledged that it is not always possible to make direct comparisons between practices adopted in different countries and that besides geographical considerations historical factors, such as tradition and infrastructure, are very important in attempting to provide any panacea solutions.

Over the last decade and against the background of rising oil prices which then existed, much discussion has centred upon means whereby more efficient use of energy resources can be realised and further interest has also been rekindled regarding the possibility of increasing the amount of refuse incineration coupled with energy recovery.

A review carried out by the Organisation for Economic Co-operation and Development in 1981 (OECD) indicated that amongst the strongest supporters of CHP were Denmark, West Germany, Italy, the Netherlands, Sweden and Austria. In the case of Denmark, approximately 30% of electricity production is associated with CHP.

In the case of the UK, according to the same report, it only amounts to about 3.5%. On a comparative basis the USA similarly has a very low percentage of electricity production associated with CHP plant although interest is increasing in this field.

In response to earlier initiatives by the Government, interest in the UK in CHP is increasing as characterised by the many studies undertaken, such as the work by W S Atkins & Partners on CHP/DH schemes and the subsequent "Lead City Schemes". (1)

Besides the less extensive use of CHP in the UK another area in which this country differs is in the extent of municipal and domestic refuse as a fuel. As a general rule it is found from experience that the amount of refuse available in an industrialised country is 400 to 500kg per capita. Hence for a population of 60 million like that of Great Britain and Northern Ireland, the total amount of domestic and municipal refuse might be expected to reach 30 million tonnes. Estimates would indicate that this is equivalent to 12 million tonnes of coal and in other terms of energy content is equivalent to 22% of all gas and oil used by industry.

It is appreciated that this hypothetical maximum cannot, in reality, be achieved for reasons associated with the logistics of delivering all the refuse throughout the country to plants at costs which are attractive to waste disposal authorities. However, there is substantial scope for increasing the amount of refuse which is incinerated in the United Kingdom since it has been estimated, at the present time, that no more than 10% of the country's domestic and commercial waste is disposed of by incineration. Of this only 3 to 5% of the total waste is incinerated in plants which are associated with energy recovery schemes. This includes both the heat recovery which is used to provide industrial process steam and district heating on the one hand and the generation of electricity on the other. In some European countries over 50% of waste is incinerated and a comparison with other countries on mainland Europe and in Scandinavia would show some striking contrasts. In particular Switzerland incinerates 65% of its domestic refuse and Denmark 75%. In both these countries the refuse is regarded primarily as a fuel rather than a waste with the result that almost all the incineration plants are associated with energy recovery.

A review of Swedish practice indicates that refuse incineration plant capacities are generally of no greater throughput than 130 000 tonnes per annum and are only associated with the provision of heat for district heating purposes.

Hence, although it is accepted that not all refuse can be made available for incineration and energy recovery, 50% may not be an unreasonable target and by this means six million tonnes of coal would be saved.

In an EEC context a European campaign "Save and Recycle our Refuse" was launched on 3 February 1984. It made the claim that if the whole of the EEC were to recover the same proportion of energy from its rubbish as Denmark does the saving would correspond to the output of 17 nuclear power stations of 1000MW capacity each.

The Atkins' Supplementary Report 3.04 on the Summary Report and Recommendations of the Stage 1 CHP/DH feasibility programme addressed the potential contribution that refuse might make to CHP schemes. It concluded that heat from refuse incineration can make a valuable contribution to large scale combined Heat & Power projects and could offer a prospect for commercially viable smaller scale district heating development.

In the context of CHP, however, it is the cogeneration of electricity and heat which is of major interest. The method of utilising refuse as a fuel in this review is primarily confined to the mass incineration of raw refuse although this is of course not the only process by which energy can be recovered. Development work is in hand on several pilot schemes in the UK to produce waste derived fuel which can be burnt in conventional boilers and further work is also required on handling, combustion, and disposal of residues. There are also several schemes in existence whereby methane gas is recovered from landfill sites.

In the USA the practice of energy recovery from waste has also been given a higher priority over the last fifteen years.

2   SYSTEM AND CONTROL ASPECTS

2.1   System Aspects

A schematic diagram of an incinerator/boiler/turbine plant is indicated in Figure 1.

Heat utilisation can take the form of electricity generation, the supply of steam for industrial processes at intermediate or low pressure, or the provision of low or high temperature hot water for district and space heating. It is possible for the heat utilisation from a single specific project to include either a combination or all of the above mentioned items. By suitable selection of the main plant components it is also possible to install a system with a high degree of flexibility whereby the ratio, between electrical generation and heat export, can be varied to accommodate particular demand requirements, thus enabling the plant to be operated to give the most economic return.

For any individual scheme the turbine can be one of three basic types. The type selected will be determined by the specific duty and flexibility of the scheme under consideration. The three types are the straight condensing machine, the back pressure machine and the

passout/condensing machine. The straight condensing steam turbine-generator would only be used in cases where there is not an immediate economic prospect of heat export in the form of low pressure steam or hot water, the only duty under consideration being the generation of electricity. The back-pressure and the passout/condensing steam turbine-generators both have advantages over the straight condensing machine in that they enable a higher steam cycle efficiency to be realised with a consequent improvement in the rate of energy conversion. The improvement in efficiency is secured by reducing the amount of low grade heat which is rejected, substantially in the form of latent heat, to the turbine condenser.

Whilst the back pressure turbine eliminates the heat loss to the condenser, it has to be noted that the system is not as flexible as for the passout/condensing turbine arrangement unless both a special steam dump and a direct supply facility are installed. The types of condenser employed are either the standard water-cooled wet system or, where there is a shortage of water, the air-cooled condenser. A higher vacuum can generally be achieved with the water-cooled condenser. To obtain such a high vacuum with an air-cooled condenser would be uneconomic and in some cases impractical.

For direct heating, either passout steam or pressure reduced steam is fed to a heat exchanger which heats the water for supplying the district heating distribution network.

In order to realise the full potential of combined heat and power schemes it is necessary to secure a high load factor for the heat exported.

Recent experience indicates that the most suitable steam generator design conditions for use in conjunction with refuse incineration and energy recovery plants are:-

Steam pressure   30 to 65 bar
Steam temperature   450°C maximum
Feedwater temperature   110 to 150°C

The design steam temperature selected is dependent upon the composition of the refuse and strongly influenced by its chemical analysis.

2.2   Control Aspects

The method of plant control associated with the operation of heat recovery boilers, turbine-generators and process steam equipment can be designed to suit the specific requirement. Generally the system would be a standard employed for that type and size of unit.

The type of incoming refuse is checked at the weigh-bridge. If bulky refuse is delivered then it would be directed for shredding or landfill, otherwise the crane operator will indicate at which gate he wants each load to be unloaded into the refuse bunker.

Control of the supply of refuse to the grates relies on skilled crane operators to ensure that a reasonable refuse mix is fed to the hoppers, so minimising the variation in the quality of refuse being fed to the boilers.

The operation and control of incineration plant falls into the category of either a semi or fully automatic system in which certain key parameters can be selected and supervised from the control room. The degree of automation varies between different manufacturers and may also be dependent upon the particular requirements of the owner and operators of each installation.

The essential conrol parameters are the steam flow, combustion temperature and excess air level. The steam flow is the key parameter for which a signal is usually taken to adjust the refuse feed rate and any variation in the selected steam flow set-point initiates a correction to the refuse feeder to restore the steam flow. The temperature in the furnace, a function of the excess air, is used to trim the secondary and primary airflows which will be adjusted either automatically or by operator action from the control room, dependent upon the particular control philosophy adopted. The grate speed can also be varied according to feed rate and furnace combustion requirements and can be performed automatically as part of the control process or by operator action from the control room.

In addition to the control of the incineration process further control functions associated with the plant involve the control of functions particular to the boiler such as drum level and steam temperature control. The operation of the turbine-generator and steam passout requirements may also form part of the overall plant control system and could, for instance, involve fixed pressure control of the turbine-generator with the provision of dump facilities in the condenser for steam over production and turbine trip conditions.

The use of mini-computers and micro-processors in the control of incineration plant has recently been introduced on a few pilot schemes incorporating optimisation techniques for efficient control of combustion.

3   TECHNICAL ASPECTS OF INCINERATOR DESIGN

The availability and successful operation of a refuse incineration CHP system requires specific attention to be given to several key factors in the plant design. In order to highlight these factors an activities diagram illustrating the principal functions involved is presented in Figure 2.

A brief description of these activities is given below.

3.1   Refuse Quantity and Analysis

The refuse quantity per annum is determined and specified in accordance with the investigations conducted during the feasibility study and economic appraisal. The chemical and physical analysis of the refuse would be determined along with the range of calorific values and then the design c.v. selected. Attention would also be given to the anticipated future trends in refuse composition during the plant life time and the plant design specified accordingly to cover an "operating window" see Figure 3.

It is important for the chemical analysis to indicate chlorine and sulphur levels in particular as they will have an important bearing on boiler design such as maximum steam conditions.

An indication of the variation in refuse quality is shown in Figure 4 and Table 1. (2) and (3).

Table 1 Refuse Analyses		1970	1983
Dust & Cinders & Screenings	%	11.8	14.8
Vegetables & Putrescible	%	34.6	19.7
Paper	%	31.9	33.8
Metal	%	6.4	6.4
Textile	%	2.3	4.2
Glass	%	9.9	9.3
Plastic	%	0.5	5.3
Unclassified	%	2.6	6.5

The analyses show how the nature of the refuse has changed over the last fifteen years or so. It can be observed how the vegetable and putrescible matter has decreased and the plastic content increased with the enhanced use of packaged foods. The calorific value has increased over the same period which not unexpectedly reflects a more affluent society.

3.2   Unacceptable Waste

Some Waste Disposal Authorities organise separate collections directly to landfill for bulky waste which the grate is incapable of accommodating. Alternatively, some plants include a shredder which can accept bulky items up to say 3 x 0.2 x 0.5m. If no separate collection is undertaken and no shredder installed, it is necessary for some prior sorting of the refuse, at the plant, to take place and arrangements made for its subsequent transportation to landfill.

3.3   Plant Outage

During plant partial outage or entire plant temporary shut down for cleaning or overhaul, normally on an annual basis, it is usually necessary to divert some refuse to landfill. Although the boiler/grate units are designed with an overload capacity this is not usually adequate to cater for the shutdown of one of the streams.

3.4   Bunker Capacity and Refuse Crane

The bunker bay is designed for the design specified refuse throughput and is sized to have adequate capacity for long weekends and bank holidays. The storage capacity is typically four days refuse at one hundred per cent design throughput. The refuse bunker also has to include sufficient capacity for the crane driver to build up a reserve of dry refuse for blending purposes. The width of the bunker will be limited by the acceptable crane span which also has to cover the width of the loading chutes. The depth of the bunker must not lead to too high a degree of compaction of the refuse.

At least two, one hundred per cent duty, cranes should be provided in order to allow for standby capacity.

3.5 Number of Units

The fundamental definition of the purpose of the plant is important. Is the primary intent refuse incineration or the export of energy in the form of heat and power? A further prominent aspect is the landfill facilities available in the event of a prolonged plant shutdown. In the case under discussion, which is combined heat and power, the variation in heat and power demands throughout the year, both seasonally and daily, will indicate the degree of flexibility required to be incorporated in the plant design. Consideration of the proven availability of various unit sizes, projected costs and planned outage periods, together with the flexibility and the guaranteed outputs required, will enable an evaluation of the number of streams to be conducted.

3.6 Design Heat Load

The design throughput at the design calorific value enables the design heat load generated in the incinerator to be established. However, consideration must be given to the range of anticipated calorific values and the overload capacity.

3.7 Refuse Throughput

Most manufacturers allow for an increased throughput level of 15 to 20%, either on a short time or continuous basis, according to specified requirements. The maximum heat load is based on this throughput at the design c.v. The c.v. range quoted is often wide, possibly 6500 to 14000KJ/kg as indicated in Figure 3.

3.8 Ash Plant

The ash plant must be capable of accepting a burden based on the maximum rate of fired throughput. The ash is of two forms, the clinker and riddlings from the grate and the fly ash which is carried over with the gases as a dust or grit burden and removed by the precipitators. The total ash is typically 35% of the initial weight of refuse throughput and 12% of the volume. The ratio of clinker and riddlings to fly ash is about 4 to 1.

The ash crane is designed to remove all the daily ash from the ash bunker in eight hours on to lorries for final removal to landfill. The ash bunker is sized to provide ample storage to cover for long weekends and bank holidays.

3.9 Precipitators

The precipitators are designed to reduce the dust burden to the level defined by the relevant authorities. The designs usually have sufficient capacity to meet these levels with half of the precipitator installation out of service.

The flue gas flow rate is determined by the maximum refuse throughput and the design excess air level required to limit the gas temperature in the furnace and convection passes to acceptable values. These values are very dependent upon the composition of the refuse as described later.

3.10 Forced Draught(F.D.) and Induced Draught (I.D.) Fans

The F.D. fans are air blowers which provide the primary and secondary air, i.e. underfire and overfire, to the grate. The I.D. fans located downstream of the precipitator directly discharge the flue gases to the chimney. All fans are rated for the maximum refuse throughput and excess air levels.

3.11 Incinerator Combustion Aspects

The mass incineration of refuse requires particular characteristics in the boiler design. Earlier designs were based upon fossil fuel fired boilers and, as such, incorporated features which subsequently resulted in numerous problems on units in various countries.

The incinerator design must be based on the principle of recovery of heat from relatively corrosive and erosive waste gases. It is essential to limit the gas temperatures entering the convection surfaces to a conservative value in comparison to a fossil fired boiler. Also it is necessary to maintain gas temperatures at the specified minimum.

It is apparent that in order to achieve high availability of steam generation from the mass burning of refuse and to eliminate earlier problems, the plant design must follow well proven techniques.

The design of a heat recovery boiler should therefore consider the following points in its design and construction:-

- High temperature problems
- Erosion of tubes
- Build-up of solids
- Initial wastage of the tube material
- Corrosion due to a reducing atmosphere
- Corrosion by chlorine
- Corrosion by sulphates
- Low temperature corrosion

Unprepared refuse is heterogeneous by nature and its characteristics vary from time to time and from place to place. Therefore high temperature problems are possible.

Studies of various refuses have indicated low ash fusion temperatures and ash high in silica and rich in alkalies, sodium and potassium. The excess air level is chosen to limit the maximum temperature in the furnace in order to maintain the temperature below the ash fusion temperature and to prevent slagging. It is dependent upon the fuel analysis. The furnace for refuse firing must be provided with ample volume to give sufficient residence time to ensure complete combustion of the fuel. Also, sufficient water cooled surface must be provided to reduce the furnace exit gas temperature to a point where the ash is not fluid and will not, therefore, freeze onto convective heating surfaces. Experience indicates that severe furnace slagging and convection fouling will occur if furnace exit temperatures are not limited to a maximum of 1000°C with temperatures into the convection zone of 700 to 800°C.

As the fly ash contains abrasive materials it is essential that, to avoid erosion damage in convective heating surfaces, the average gas velocity should be limited to an acceptable value.

To avoid bridging by deposits between tubes in convective heating surfaces, it is necessary to provide widely spaced tubes, in line, especially in the high gas temperature zones. It is essential that only plain tubes should be used for all heat recovery surfaces. The important principle of design should be an arrangement of tubes to achieve a maximum efficiency of cleaning either by long retractable sootblowers, sonic sootblowers or by rapping gear to vibrate pendant elements. The use of rapping gear allows a small protective ash layer to remain on the tubes so reducing corrosion problems in the lower temperature areas of the boiler.

Very early failures of low metal temperature heating surfaces located at the furnace exit have occurred. Investigations have shown that an initial reaction takes place between the chloride content of the flue gas, primarily as hydrogen chloride and to some extent the alkali chlorides, and the steel surfaces before protective oxides or sulphate films can form. To avoid this problem initial firing should be by refuse having a low chloride content in the flue gas thus allowing a protective film to form on the tubes.

Corrosion of furnace tubes can be caused by the products of partial combustion in a reducing atmosphere. Local reducing conditions can exist, even with very high excess air levels, due to stratification and/or incorrect air and/or fuel distribution. In this way carbon monoxide and hydrogen sulphide can be produced which attack furnace tubing and cause failure. Chlorine corrosion results from chlorine and hydrogen chloride, the chlorine being introduced by the plastic materials in the refuse.

The heavy metals, lead and zinc, in the form of chlorides of lead, and sulphates and chlorides of zinc, contribute to corrosion at high metal temperature levels.

Stainless steel tubes with residual manufacturing stresses, e.g. at bends, may also be prone to stress corrosion cracking and/or corrosion fatigue in the presence of gaseous chlorides.

To avoid these problems, correct metal temperatures must be determined and the heating surfaces designed to suit. Additionally optimum use of the tube cleaning facilities must be made.

Corrosion by sulphates has been observed on austenitic steel superheater tubes. Investigations have revealed very high amounts of alkali, about 20% by weight of sodium and potassium, and negligible amounts of chlorine in the deposits. One of the solutions to this problem would be the use of ferritic steels for the superheater, the final steam temperature being limited to a conservative value.

Low temperature corrosion occurs when the flue gas contacts surfaces which are at temperatures below the dew point of the corrosive constituents of the flue gases. It is important in the design of the plant that the low temperature corrosion problem should be considered for the design of ducting, i.d. fans, precipitators and stack, as failure of plant in these areas would obviously lead to outages.

Three important considerations must be catered for in the design of the convection pass heating surfaces in addition to the normal heat transfer requirements.

(a) Limitation of erosion of tubes by reducing the gas velocity.

(b) Selection of correct metal temperatures to prevent corrosion. Selection of tube material and wall thicknesses in relation to long term life.

(c) Correct design of tube pitching to prevent fouling and, at the same time, permit satisfactory tube cleaning.

It is essential that all tubes be designed for optimum cleaning whether this be by means of sootblowers, sonic blowers or vibration of the elements.

3.12 Incinerator Grates

The incinerator grate manufacturer is normally responsible for the combustion process and because of this will have a substantial input into the design of the heat recovery section, working in conjunction with the boiler manufacturer.

A typical scheme for feeding raw refuse into an incinerator is to push the refuse, by means of a hydraulic ram, usually on to some form of agitating grate. This is necessary in order to turn the refuse over to ensure complete combustion.

A grate area is designed to be conservatively loaded, even under overload conditions. The primary air is fed under the grate to facilitate cooling.

Several styles of grates are employed and arranged in various ways in order to perform the agitating action.

3.13 Boiler Efficiency

The boiler efficiency increases as the temperature into the precipitator decreases. However, if the temperature is too low there is a danger of corrosion due to the corrosive nature of the exhaust gases and "dew-point" associated problems. The temperature range is usually 220 to 300°C, and a boiler efficiency of 75% at an exhaust temperature of 250°C into the precipitator is typical.

3.14 Steam Conditions

Design pressures associated with refuse incineration heat recovery plant vary between 30 and 65 bar with temperatures essentially limited by the constituents of the combustion gases.

Steam temperatures are often kept low if the chlorine content of the fuel is high. The temperature range is normally 350 to 450°C and attempts are generally made to use standard pressures for the steam plant i.e. 35, 40 and 65 bar.

3.15 Boiler Heating Surface Design

The basic design heat load is determined by the design refuse throughput and the design calorific value whilst the maximum heat load is based on maximum refuse throughput and the design calorific value - See Figure 3.

The heating surface area must be conservatively designed to accommodate the maximum heat load and prevent an unacceptable rise in the tube metal temperatures and in the flue gas temperature into the precipitator.

The gas flows and temperatures are determined by the excess air level and maximum throughput. The excess air level is of paramount importance in limiting the corrosion and slagging implications.

The heating surfaces are designed with tube pitching to limit gas velocities to between 5 and 7 m/sec. Designs also often allow for heat transfer to be reduced by a layer of dust up to a certain thickness.

3.16 Steam Air Heaters

Steam air heater facilities are provided for use when the refuse has a high moisture content and also for cases of low ambient air temperatures. Typically the facilities enable primary air temperatures of 120 to 150°C to be achieved under all anticipated operating conditions.

3.17 Plant Performance and Guarantees

In order for the manufacturer or contractor responsible for the design of the incinerator grate/boiler unit to guarantee its performance it is necessary for the following aspects to be covered by the purchaser's specification or clearly stated by the contractor.

(a) A range of refuse calorific values with which the plant is to operate satisfactorily during its design life time.

(b) The refuse design calorific value, its ultimate analysis and the design throughput for which the steam generated output shall be guaranteed.

(c) The grate design refuse throughput and its overload capacity together with an indication of the overload time scale.

(d) The minimum steam output to be achieved with the design refuse throughput and design calorific value with specified steam conditions, feed temperature and ambient air temperature. The contractor will be required to guarantee the actual nett steam generated, i.e., after deduction for steam air heating or steam sootblowing, at the specified steam conditions with a boiler only in the "on-load" cleaned condition at the end of the trial run.

(e) The specification will normally also specify the maximum and minimum allowable gas temperatures at exit from the economiser or into the precipitator and the contractor is required to give the actual temperature under the stated design conditions. This point effectively defines the boiler efficiency together with the complete combustion guarantees, i.e., the unburnt carbon, charred paper and putrescible matter in the ash and the radiation and unaccounted losses.

(f) The required full load performance of the precipitator will be stated with reference to the allowable dust burden at a specified O_2 or CO_2 level.

(g) The contractor will be required to state and guarantee the achievable operating hours between outages for off-load cleaning necessitated by the incinerator failing to generate the minimum guaranteed steam flow or of exceeding the maximum allowable temperature into the precipitator. The contractor will also be required to define the outage period per annum for maintenance, overhaul or off-load cleaning and the means by which on-load cleaning will be facilitated. These data establish the anticipated unit availability.

The auxiliary power absorbed by the plant associated with the incinerator grate/boiler unit must be stated by the contractor.

The contractor must define the minimum boiler load, for stable operation, at which the unit can continuously operate and guarantee that it meets the requirements of the purchaser.

Finally it is acknowledged that the above list may not be sufficiently exhaustive to meet the requirements of all owners or operators of refuse incineration plants. Some owners may require guarantees to be given and tested at several points of the "operating window" and not just at the minimum, design and overload steam loads. Further, some continental operators require the plant to be tested at the end of the continuous operation period with the boiler only in the "on-load" cleaned condition after say 8,000 hours rather than in the clean condition appertaining at the end of the trial run.

4 ECONOMIC ASPECTS

In determining the viability of a new project involving refuse mass incineration and CHP the financial assessment involves many diverse factors. A Waste Disposal Authority (WDA) or its successor, considers the option in comparison with the availability and cost of landfill operations which may also be linked with the collection and sale of methane gas from the landfill sites. In addition to the cost of alternative disposal methods, the viability of a particular scheme is influenced by the scale of operation of the plant. This again is primarily influenced by the amount of refuse which can be made available and its associated disposal fee payable to the plant, the heat demand which may be in the form of process steam or district heating, the prices of alternative conventional fuels and the electricity tariffs at which the Electricity Supply Industry (ESI) will purchase the electricity. The required degree of penetration into the market for heat make it imperative that the heat price should have a competitive edge against the cost of generation of heat from other fuels. Further it may be necessary for the heat supplier to ensure that the customer is provided with adequate standby facilities in the event of the steam generation from the incineration plant not being available.

Some recent studies in the UK have indicated that, for a refuse fired CHP plant of economic size and operating at a constant throughput, the income from the sale of heat and electricity is approximately the same irrespective of the ratio of the heat to electricity exported. The income, however, is sensitive to the price of heat determined by competition with conventional heat only plants hence, in order to accommodate changes in the structure of heat and electricity prices over the life of the plant, it is clearly advantageous to have installed a plant which incorporates a high degree of flexibility. Further the inclusion of heat storage facilities also aids flexibility of operation since the peak demands for heat and electricity often coincide.

From a conservation of primary fuel standpoint the operation of the plant in the CHP mode is more beneficial than electricity only.

Operated as an electricity only installation the plant efficiency is low compared to a modern power station and the capital cost per kilowatt high.

The size of the plant, the refuse disposal fees, a high load factor together with a high plant availability are of major importance if the project is to prove attractive to the private investor. (4)

The availability of the mass refuse incineration process with energy recovery is now considered to be well proven. (5)

In Europe and Scandinavia the practice adopted is to predominantly regard the refuse as a fuel and, where possible, in the first place, to operate in conjunction with existing heating schemes. Electrical generation is normally a secondary consideration.

In the UK the Energy Act 1983 required the ESI to purchase electricity from private generators and to also support and adopt CHP. However, at the present time, there is much debate regarding the level of the purchase tariffs for the electricity.

In the USA the Public Utilities Regulatory Policies Act (PURPA) was passed in 1978 and since then, according to some sources, the installation of CHP plant has more than doubled

and in 1984 was estimated to be about 7% of the US electricity production.

Additionally, the field of planned refuse incineration coupled with electricity production is increasing considerably e.g. in New York, New England and Chicago.

In the UK, in view of the different standpoints from which a WDA and private investor may regard a project i.e. landfill average disposal costs compared to an internal rate of return, a new initiative to reconcile the interests may be necessary.

The approximate current costs for a refuse fired CHP plant of 450 000 tonnes per annum throughput can be anticipated as up t £50 million for capital costs and £7 per tonne of annual throughput for operating and maintenance costs.

5   ENVIRONMENTAL IMPACT AND FUTURE LEGISLATION

Environmental conditions must be considered from several other standpoints apart from the discharge of waste gases and their constituents via the chimney; namely noise levels both external and internal to the plant, the avoidance of objectionable odours and the effect of road vehicles on traffic conditions and local inhabitants.

The criteria for determining the permissible and acceptable levels for emissions are established by local regulations and national standards. However, in addition to these when considering the installation of any long term plant, due deference should be given to the present "climate of opinion" regarding emissions and the Directive which is to be issued by the European Commission on Combating Air Pollution from Industrial Plants. The requirements of this Directive are to be implemented by June 1987 and their effects could be significant for new and possibly existing plants. Although the SO_x amd NO_x emissions are not as prominent as for fossil fired stations, dust and grit factors are present and are also accompanied by the emission of HCl, HF, gases and slight traces of dioxin.

With regard to waste gases being discharged up the chimney and the heterogeneous nature of the refuse fuel together with the manner in which it is burned (i.e., considerable agitation, coupled with the high ash content), the particulate quantity will be high - figures of up to 11 g/m^3 in combustion gases can be expected. United Kingdom regulations regarding grit emissions to the atmosphere require a limit of 0.115 g/Nm^3. From practical experience it is possible to limit emissions to approximately 0.05 g/Nm^3 by installing electrostatic precipitators of satisfactory design. With the large amounts of excess air (up to 100%) necessary, there are large volumes of nitrogen present in the combustion process. However, because of the relatively low furnace temperature the production of NO_x is low. The sulphur content of the fuel is low and emissions of SO_x should not present undue problems, unless of course the refuse is mixed with lower grade high sulphur fuels.

In certain locations, because of the limitations imposed by the Authorities, high cost wet or dry flue gas scrubbing and treatment may be necessary to remove traces of the chloride and fluoride gases.

From studies made up to the present time dioxin emissions from incineration plants in Sweden appear to be approximately $0.5ng/m^3$ gas of 2, 3, 7, 8 TCDD. (6)

It is possible that there is a relationship between dioxin emissions and combustion temperature. The Swedish National Board of Environmental Protection requires, in spirit at least, that in all applications for permission to incinerate refuse, the entire flue gas volume must be at a temperature of 800°C minimum leaving the furnace.

The Swedish requirements are a minimum of $50mg/Nm^3$ for emitted dust particles and many of their refuse incineration plants produce considerably lower levels than this.

The carbon monoxide (CO) content in the flue gas is a direct measurement of the plant combustion efficiency. When the CO value is less than $100-250mg/Nm^3$ the emissions are also normally slight.

Continuous operation of plant, by experienced staff, helps to reduce emissions and on and off firing by other fuels such as combustion support oil is also beneficial.

Noise levels are generally controlled by enclosing the plant in a suitably designed and constructed building and installing machinery which is in accordance with the best international standards.

Objectionable odours are suppressed by virtue of careful design, whereby the refuse bunker bay forms an enclosure within the main building and the combustion air is ducted from the top of the bunkers. The ash is sterile and moist with no putrescible matter present and therefore no problems arise from the use of open ash bays.

Experience has shown that noise from refuse collection vehicles need not **present** a problem providing the approach to the bunker apron is suitably designed and allowable vehicle speeds are limited.

The plant must be located so that access for refuse vehicles does not cause undue congestion to existing traffic.

6   CONCLUSIONS

The results of the review indicate that the availabilities of refuse fired CHP plant are well proven and that in the UK the incentive to install them rests mainly upon economic factors which tend to be assessed in isolation.

In some countries the refuse is treated as a fuel which can be used to aid the conservation of primary fuels.

The environmental problems associated with refuse plant do not appear to be unsurmountable providing the degree of correct equipment is installed.

7   ACKNOWLEDGEMENTS

The author wishes to thank the Partners of Kennedy & Donkin for permission to publish this paper; also to my colleagues within Kennedy & Donkin for their assistance, particularly Mr. H.A. Kirby for his encouragement and Mr. C.R. Dracup for his considerable effort in helping with the preparation of the text.

REFERENCES

(1)   W.S. Atkins and Partners.   1982 CHP/DH Feasibility Programme. Stage 1.   Summary Report and Recommendations.

(2)   A.E. Higginson.   The Analysis of Domestic Waste. IWM Publication No.10 June 1982.

(3)   J.H.S. Smart. IEE 11th Annual Meeting on the History of Electrical Engineering. 16th July 1983.

(4)   R.J. Perrett.   Economic Incentives for Recovering Energy from Refuse. Seminar on Energy Recovery from Refuse Incineration. I.Mech.E February 1985.

(5)   N. Barnes.   Operational Performance of Waste-to-Energy Plants.   Seminar on Energy Recovery from Refuse Incineration. I.Mech.E February 1985.

(6)   Warmer Bulletin - September 1985.

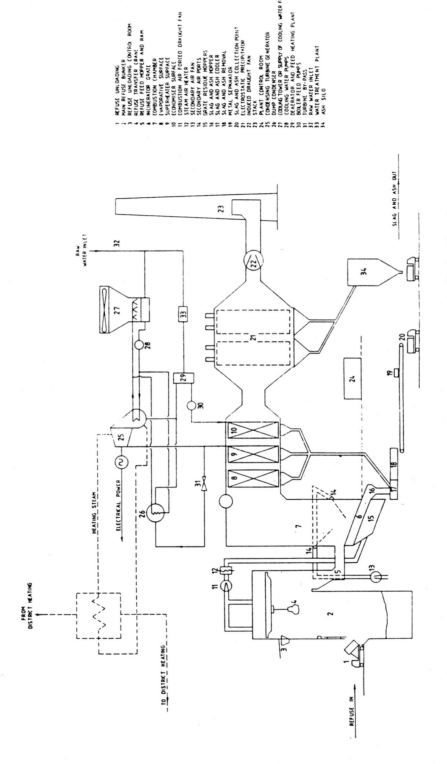

1 REFUSE UNLOADING
2 MAIN REFUSE BUNKER
3 REFUSE UNLOADING CONTROL ROOM
4 REFUSE TRANSFER CRANE
5 REFUSE FEED HOPPER AND RAM
6 INCINERATOR GRATE
7 COMBUSTION CHAMBER
8 EVAPORATIVE SURFACE
9 SUPERHEATER SURFACE
10 ECONOMISER SURFACE
11 COMBUSTION AIR FORCED DRAUGHT FAN
12 STEAM AIR HEATER
13 SECONDARY AIR FAN
14 SECONDARY AIR PORTS
15 GRATE RESIDUE HOPPERS
16 SLAG AND ASH HOPPER
17 SLAG AND ASH COOLER
18 SLAG AND ASH REMOVAL
19 METAL SEPARATOR
20 SLAG AND ASH COLLECTION POINT
21 ELECTROSTATIC PRECIPITATOR
22 INDUCED DRAUGHT FAN
23 STACK
24 PLANT CONTROL ROOM
25 CONDENSING TURBINE GENERATOR
26 DUMP CONDENSER
27 COOLING TOWER OR SUPPLY OF COOLING WATER FROM RIVER
28 COOLING WATER PUMPS
29 DEAERATOR AND FEED HEATING PLANT
30 BOILER FEED PUMPS
31 TURBINE BY-PASS
32 RAW WATER INLET
33 WATER TREATMENT PLANT
34 ASH SILO

Fig 1   Schematic diagram of incinerator/boiler/turbine plant

9

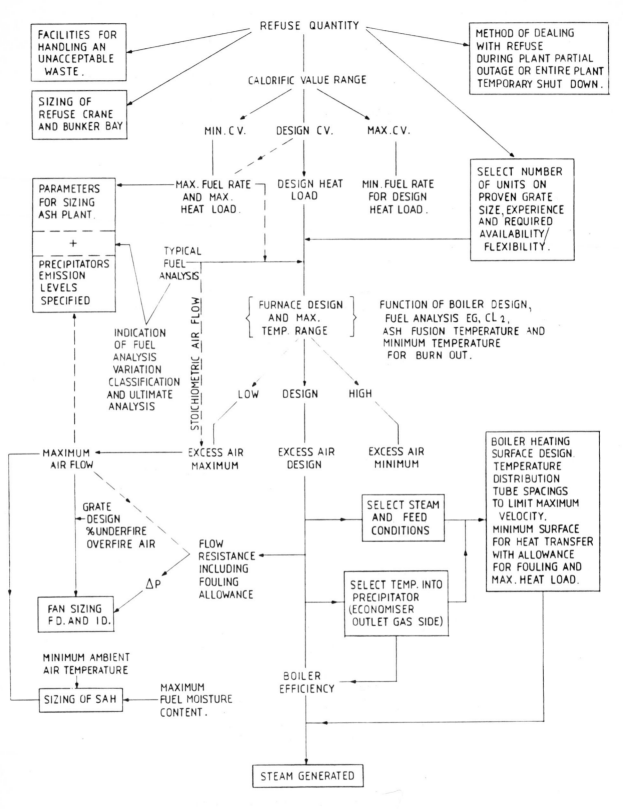

Fig 2   Activities diagram

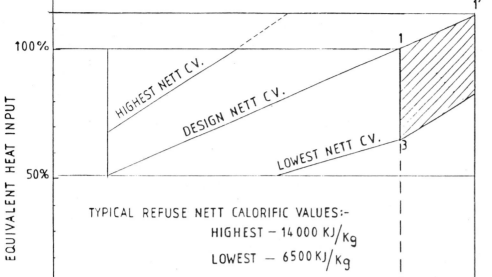

Fig 3   Typical incinerator operating window (for heat input)

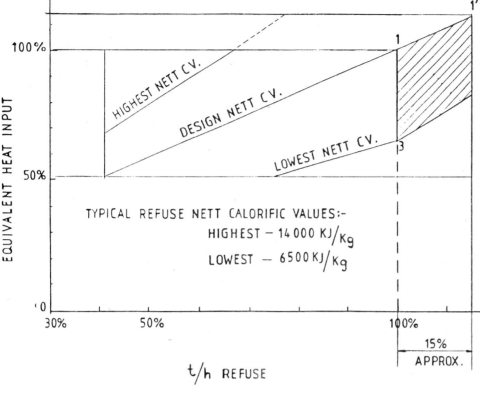

Fig 4   Typical incinerator operating envelope (for calorific value)

The performance of Moscow's district heating system - technical, economic, and organisational factors

H RYDING, BSc, MCIBSE, MInstE, CEng
Department of Civil Engineering and Construction, Aston University

SYNOPSIS
The paper describes the two district heating systems in Moscow, with details of plant and operation, as well as the different economic conditions under which they operate. Efficiency comparisons are made with Swedish and West German schemes. There are some successes in integration of CHP plant into the regional grid, and the difficulties involved in planning and coordination between electricity utility, local authority and construction company, when the system is expanding, are discussed.

1   INTRODUCTION

We may begin by asking what may we learn from Moscow? It may be argued that under such different political and economic conditions, the difficulties of making appropriate cost conversions, and the inherent language difficulties, little can be learnt that is useful to Western engineers. This does not seem to me to be the case, for a number of reasons.

First of all, it must be said that there is so little published on the **operation** of **existing** schemes, (as opposed to the feasibility of **new** schemes), that for this reason alone, recent Soviet sources* prove a welcome addition to the technical literature. Moscow's centralised heat supply scheme has been developed since 1924, and as the largest scheme in the world, is considered a show-piece of Soviet achievement. Very little of CHP/dh technology is new or "high tech". The USSR has a good reputation for its technology in the related field of electricity supply. We would not expect significant technical differences from Western practice here, and if they do occur, that of itself will be interesting.

The political and economic objections are less important when considering heat and electricity supply, than for other industries. All CHP/district heating schemes involve some form of public ownership and control, because of their public utility nature. After the oil crisis of the 1970s, there has been increasing state intervention in the market for fuel, both in protecting national fuel interests, and in providing investment for energy conservation.

----

* Information is drawn from a considerably longer paper on Moscow, forming part of the author's forthcoming doctoral thesis. Detailed references have not been included, for reasons of space, but the main bibliographical sources are listed at the end of the paper.

The current climate of "economic efficiency" and privatisation is making us reconsider our attitudes to public enterprise, and investigations of other countries' public utilities and their performance may clarify and stimulate our own ideas. The organisation of Moscow's centralised heat supply with the involvement of both the electricity utility and the City Council has potential interest for our own proposed CHP consortia. Improved efficiency, energy conservation and increased output from the same input of resources are increasingly important goals for the Soviet economy, as growth rates slow down, just as for this country.

As already mentioned, there has been little evaluation of schemes actually in operation. Does CHP/dh actually produce the savings claimed for it or justify the large capital investments involved? What are the correct measures of efficiency? Early attempts by Lind and Thörnqvist to compare the performance of Swedish and German schemes show that this is not a simple task.

This paper discusses some technical and organisational aspects of Moscow's centralised heat supply system, with a view to making some assessment of its effectiveness, compared with other countries' schemes. Since most readers will not be familiar with Moscow and its economic conditions, a brief description is given first.

2   MOSCOW

In 1985, 8.6 million people lived within Moscow city's administrative area (886 km2) and thus it ranks in size with London and Paris. Moscow lies in latitude 55°N, with a heating season of 205 days, and an outside design temperature of -25°C.

[handwritten note: Compare with Glasgow 56°N or West Coast heating season - outside temp 25°C]

In the Moscow region, there is a limited supply of local wood, peat and hydroelectric power, supplemented by lignite from the Moscow coal field. This coal costs roughly twice as much as coal from sources at least 1000km away, and several times as much as Volga oil (700 km from Moscow) or Stavropol gas (1100 km). Pipeline transport of fuel is thus preferred and also relieves the transport system (predominantly rail) which is heavily congested. Moscow acquires electricity from the local power board which is linked into the national grid bringing power from the huge hydroelectric stations in Siberia.

All the State departments, ministries, research, planning and construction institutes are concentrated in Moscow. There is also a strong industrial base, producing 25% of all machinery, tools, electrical equipment,and railway vehicles; 50% of all motor vehicles; and over 75% of all textile goods and books. Much of the industry is concentrated in very large plants, often with their own boilerhouses.

Moscow, like the rest of the Soviet Union, suffered from a severe housing shortage during the period of industrialisation 1930-1950. In the late 50s this began to be remedied, and by 1966, two-fifths of Moscow´s entire housing space consisted of identical 5-storey blocks constructed using rapid assembly of standardised prefabricated concrete sections. This policy yielded relatively low density housing, which was comparatively costly to service with water, gas, electricity, heat, transport and refuse collection. By 1971, 8-16 storey (or higher) buildings provided 39% of all Moscow´s housing space, compared with 20% in 1966. It is difficult to grasp the rate at which new housing has been constructed in Moscow. During 1961-65, the total new housing constructed was 5,565,000m2 or at 9m2/person, housing for 618,000 people, -- a ´middlesized´ British city like Newcastle, or Sheffield. Between 1958 and 1970, about 5 million people had been rehoused in new flats.

3   REASONS FOR CHP/DH DEVELOPMENT

Some of the essential preconditions favouring the adoption of CHP/dh therefore exist in Moscow, namely expensive, low-grade fuel, and a large high density heat load, both industrial and domestic. Although the fuels used now, are oil and gas, when CHP/dh was originally considered in the 1920s, the comparisons were made between low grade brown coal, or peat, fired in power stations or large boiler houses, and firewood on domestic stoves brought in by cart or rail. Additional advantages were the increased efficiency of combustion, and hence reduced pollution.

However, an overwhelming reason for the establishment of CHP in the 1920s and 30s was the drive for electrification. Most factories in Europe were in the process of changing from steam to electricity, and the Soviet Union was far behind in this process. Electricity generation was much less efficient and, for industrial enterprises, electricity was a often useful by-product of heat generation rather than vice-versa. When electrification was a primary requirement for industrialisation, any

technology which reduced fuel consumption, at the same time as producing electricity, was likely to be adopted as a very important step forward. In more modern times, CHP/dh has continued to be economic because the fuel and transport saving has offset the cost of extending mains networks, and the cost of new power stations.

4   ORGANISATION

Moscow´s centralised heat system is run by two separate utilities; one fed mainly by CHP and the other fed entirely by boiler houses. They have been built and are managed separately, and until 1965 were not physically linked. They are described separately below, but first we must explain their organisation.

Electricity supply, transmission and some distribution is the responsibility of the Ministry of Power and Electrification (Minenergo). Because of the early importance of electrification, and the large investments required in the technology, it has become a very powerful and influential Ministry, able to exert the necessary pressures to ensure it receives a large share of national investment. Although all economic decisions are theoretically made by the central planners, in practice, it would appear that Minenergo is given output targets for heat and electricity, and quotas of turbines and pipework, and then left to get on with most of the planning itself. The Ministry has its own design and construction institutes which draw up heat plans, and design new systems, and its own construction organisations to carry them out. There are regional power boards of which the one for the Moscow area is Mosenergo. Within Mosenergo are separate units, run on what we would call "commercial" lines, (ie expected to make a profit, or at least cover their costs), operating individual power stations, the heat and electricity networks, and repair services. Salaries and wages of all the staff are supplemented by bonuses, (often large percentages of salaries), which are paid for achievement of performance targets, according to various formulae. One of the goals of the Soviet government has been to gear these bonuses to greater efficiency, labour productivity, and profitability in general. This has proved especially difficult in the case of heat and power, as we shall see later.

The supply of heat from CHP therefore comes directly from the regional power board. Investment decisions on CHP plant are made directly by the Ministry, and the CHP plant is integrated with other generating plant. Power and heat is also purchased from industrial stations, whose plant operates under the control of the Mosenergo load dispatchers. There is thus no external conflict of interest between an electricity utility and a heat utility. This is not to say there may not be some conflict internally within the Ministry, when electricity turns out to be more profitable than heat!

The second heat utility, Teploenergiya forms part of the Moscow City Council. Like many continental municipalities, (and like British cities before nationalisation), Moscow City Council has departments operating water, sewerage, gas, and telephone systems, (and some electricity distribution). It must also ensure fuel supplies within the city, for heating, (both supply and distribution) and monitor pollution; and hence has an interest in providing district heating, as well as operating heating systems within the housing it operates.

However, local government does not have access to the same central funds as the Ministry of Power. It has not acquired the same prestige, and quality in housing has only recently become a priority. Although Moscow City Council is similar in power and influence to the GLC, the housing and communal services budget is still similarly constrained by the grant from central government according to the priorities laid down by them, and reflected in the priorities set up by local government officials.

In considering heat supply from the point of the Moscow end-user there is also an intermediary "landlord". Although in Moscow most housing belongs to the City Council, industrial enterprises also provide housing for their workers (eg Mosenergo provides some of its own housing). Since the landlord operates and maintains the local distribution system on "his" estate, he can appear as the heat supplier to the individual flat dweller. This can lead to confusion over responsibilities, particularly over repairs, and also problems when trying to establish incentives for energy conservation.

4   HEAT PLANNING

By this we mean the physical planning of the organisation of heat production and distribution in an area. While the Soviet central planners will determine what types of solutions are possible or allowable, by determining overall production of plant and material, and levels of investment, this will not be decided down to the detail necessary to plan the projects in the Moscow area. Although we know that the central planners have determined the conditions under which CHP will generally be economic, it is the local decision-makers who will produce a scheme. However, as in the West, this requires the integration of many individual demands for heat, and many investment decisions, and this is no easier to do in the USSR, than in the West, if decisions are taken bureaucratically, or delayed at a higher level.

The actual mechanism for heat planning in Moscow is not clear. Both Mosenergo and Moscow City Council will have to plan heat supply for their own areas of responsibility. Either could operate a distribution system, but electricity generation is planned and operated only by Mosenergo. Some coordination and cooperation will obviously be necessary, in new areas of the city. It is clear from accounts of how the two networks were developed, that this coordination and cooperation was not automatic and has taken considerable time to build up, and would involve some bargaining on both sides.

When the massive housing construction programme began, serious problems arose in the sequencing of the construction of heating plant, housing construction and the heating network. Between 1951 and 1960, although there was spare capacity in CHP stations Nos. 12 and 16, this could not be used, since there were no heating mains built. This also applied to CHP station No. 22, which operated for several years but could not supply heat to the area it was to serve. These programming and construction failures were blamed on the City Council's inadequately qualified staff, who were out of their depth on such a huge project; and on inadequate funding of utilities as a proportion of the total housing budget.

Heating for the new housing was at first provided in a piecemeal way. Temporary boilerhouses were constructed, working on coal or oil, and later on gas, for those areas eventually to be fed from the CHP network. Areas outside the CHP region were also fed by small boilerhouses. The size of the boilerhouses began at about 3.5-11.6MW, serving groups of buildings, but later it became necessary to build boilerhouses for whole districts and regions, with heat loads of 11.6-60MW. A 35MW regional boilerhouse could serve a "microregion" with a population up to 20,000 people.

In an attempt to control this spread of boilerhouses, Moscow was divided up into three zones: one fed by the CHP network; one fed by the district heating network; and one fed by small boilerhouses, eventually all to be gas-fired. The zoning envisaged that in the period 1961-65, 14 regional boilerhouses would be built with a total capacity of 2400MW, and also 70 steam boilerhouses, (presumably for local industry). The construction of this network was justified by a saving of 3 million roubles. 1400 small boilers were to be changed over to gas, and up to 3600 small boilers would be eliminated. Altogether, 5 million tons of solid fuel were eliminated from the city's fuel supply, and more than 17,000 maintenance and operating personnel were no longer needed. This plan formed the basis for the establishment of Teploenergiya in 1961.

The construction of mains also did not go smoothly. Mosenergo failed to construct some of the transmission mains on time, and work had to be subcontracted out. In this case, inexperience could not be the excuse, and this directly affected Mosenergo's own output and use of plant.

At the same time one should remember that some of the large regional boilerhouses were originally intended to be temporary measures until pipelines were built to the CHP station. The CHP stations already contained an equivalent heat capacity in the turbines or peak boilers. Thus some of the plant was beingunnecessarily duplicated. The Western practice of planning boilerhouses dispersed throughout the network, to be used as temporary heat sources while loads build up, and then to be used as peak boiler or reserve capacity, is not always adopted by Soviet designers, (possibly because of too optimistic programming), but may also be due to Mosenergo designers' desire to concentrate all its plant in one place, wherever possible, and to avoid direct involvement in housing programmes.

By 1979, the division of Moscow into CHP/non-CHP networks was breaking down. Boilerhouses have been transfered to Mosenergo and the networks linked. This enables

Teploenergiya to shut down plant in the summer for maintenance while increasing the heat load on the turbines at a period of low load. Moscow network engineers seemed in favour of this, since it moved closer to their ideal of a single management structure. In 1979, difficulties had arisen when Teploenergiya had built up heat loads big enough to justify the construction of the new Southern CHP station, but the electrical load had not matched this and Mosenergo did not begin operating this station till 1983.

Although some unification has been possible, it is not clear which Ministry should have overall control. Mosenergo would not want to take on all the local distribution systems which are often poorly maintained and operated by their "landlords", (which might be feasibly be run by Teploenergiya), nor would it be willing to give up power station heat supply. This has left something of a stalemate.

5 MOSENERGO HEAT AND POWER BOARD

In 1977 this system was fed by 14 CHP stations, of which 6 supplied steam, for industrial use, and all provided hot water. Because Moscow is a hilly city, 22 pumping stations are required. The network is divided into 12 operational regions, each with its own control centre with remote sensing and control of plant, and a large central control centre provides overall load dispatching and control. In 1977 2290km of hot water mains served 33,500 buildings and 500 industrial factories, and there were a further 75 km of steam mains. Mains sizes ranged from 100mm up to 1400mm dia for hot water and up to 700mm dia for steam.

In 1975, 73.6% of the heat load of Moscow's housing and community buildings, and 32.8% of the industrial heat load was met by the CHP network. An idea of the growth of the network can be obtained from Table 1. Between 1960 and 1980, the electrical and heat capacity have grown by a factor of five, as has the heat output, while the number of stations has grown from 10 to 13.

5.1 Stations

Figure 1 shows the siting of the CHP stations. The oldest station, No.1, is sited on an island in the river Moskva in the very centre of Moscow near Red Square and the Kremlin. This station was originally a condensing station, but was converted and supplying heat by 1931, to the area within the Garden Ring, (see Figure 1). No. 1 station has been re-equipped several times and in 1977 had an electrical capacity of 500 MW. Recent details of most stations described below are given in Table 3.

Outside this ring, the CHP stations are closely based on industrial areas, being originally power stations attached to large plants. Stations No. 7 and 8 also date from the 1930s and in 1976 were being re-equipped. Station No. 9 was based at the All-Union Thermotechnical Institute (VTI). This station has been used as a research station since 1930. The ZIL automobile plant, in this area, also has its own CHP station, the largest factory CHP station in Moscow.

Station No. 11 is situated in an industrial area to the east. By 1940 it had a 200MW heat load. The 1950s saw an expansion of capacity in the West (stations 12 and 16). The first large main under the river was laid in a metal tunnel, from station No. 12. In this period the older parts of the city were connected to the networks. Spare capacity in these last two stations was available for the housing expansion. Station 20, sited near Moscow University and the new housing areas in the south-west, was the last station to be sited within the city. Station 20 also took over some of the more central load previously fed by stations No. 12 and 16.

The next series of CHP stations (Nos. 21, 22, 23, 25, and Southern), were all built on the outskirts of Moscow, (13-15km from the centre), and are generally sited near industrial enterprises, eg. No. 22 next to an oil refinery. Difficulties occurred in finding sites for the stations, and they were banished to the outer ring road to reduce pollution. Mains are being gradually extended from the outer ring stations to take load from the central areas, so that these may in turn be redeveloped and fed from the re-equipped central stations.

It can thus be seen that CHP stations have generally been sited near the industrial loads they serve, and then mains are gradually extended in radius to cover these less dense heat loads.

6 TEPLOENERGIYA DISTRICT HEATING UTILITY

In 1979, this group of networks had 24 district boilerhouses and 20 regional boilerhouses, with a total heat capacity of 6000MW, 270km of trunk mains, 460km of distribution mains, and 450 heat substations. This fed 7500 buildings, or 16-17% of buildings connected to heating networks. Some further details are shown in Table 4.

7 MAINS NETWORKS AND CONSUMER CONNECTIONS

Moscow's heating networks are of the usual two pipe closed system type, for hot water. The open system, where domestic hot water is drawn directly from the heating mains, and often described in Soviet literature, does not occur in Moscow.

Until the early 1960s most buildings had individual connections to the mains, with jet pumps providing the mixing control. Heat meters are installed for some industrial and communal buildings. Heating charges for housing are based on a flat rate according to the floor area of the dwelling, and the City Council would appear to buy heat wholesale from the CHP network. Neither radiator valves nor heat meters are generally available for domestic heating.

Heat substations have been introduced to solve some of the control and metering problems this causes. Their use began in 1960, and they were designed to serve a number of housing blocks. The optimal size of a heat substation is 23-35MW (or about the same size as one of the original group or district boilerhouses).

8 PERFORMANCE

While different countries will invest different amounts on systems, and will justify this with different financial and fuel savings, the usage of the network and plant should be similar if an effective investment has been made. Performance indicators such as those shown in Table 2 can thus be compared for different countries.

Two sources are used for comparison. Lind has provided indicators averaged over all Swedish public district heating schemes for 1972/3 to 1976/77. Thörnqvist has analysed other indicators over a similar period for West German and Swedish district heating companies. There are obvious difficulties in drawing conclusions from such a small set of figures for Moscow, but some interesting points arise.

Lind has shown that although one might expect a variation in the utilisation time for heat load with degree days, this did not occur in the Swedish figures he examined. Utilisation times ranged from 1748 to 1890 hours. The Moscow figures are considerably higher, usually around 3000 hours. Lind notes that different countries use different definitions of connected load, and this can affect utilisation times significantly. It has not been possible to establish exactly how Moscow's connected load is defined. He also notes that for a system undergoing significant expansion, utilisation times using connected load at the end of the year will be shorter. This makes Moscow's high figures remarkable. Lind gives figures for specific length ranging from 75 to 175 m/GWh, for 80% of Swedish systems, and 400m/GWh for the Danish city of Odense, as an example of low density heat load. Moscow's specific length has been falling from 48m/GWh in 1945 to 35 m/GWh in 1981. Some reduction would be expected as the heat load increasingly incorporates housing as well as industrial heat. Nevertheless this low figure needs explanation. Some possibilities are: relatively high heat load, possibly caused by the climate; high heat load densities, caused by the type of housing construction; relatively wasteful energy usage in high mains losses, poor insulation, poor space heating control. All these possibilities can be justified by Soviet sources, but it is difficult to establish which is most significant without further research. From the discussion of organisation above, it may well be that Mosenergo functions as a bulk supplier of heat, operating mainly transmission mains. This would be borne out by the fact that its parent Ministry claims responsibility for only 10% of all heating mains, nationally.

In another study, Thörnqvist has shown that low heat delivery ratios (TJ/km, the inverse of specific length), can lead to operating losses in Swedish systems. Moscow figures have increased from 74 TJ/km in 1945 to 103 TJ/km in 1981, compared with Swedish ranges of 10-60 TJ/km with the larger figures corresponding with the larger systems (up to 10,000 TJ/a). West German figures given by Thörnqvist ranged from 10-50 TJ/km for outputs up to 4000TJ/a. For the Moscow output of 202,230 TJ/a, the higher heat delivery ratios would therefore not be surprising.

The latest performance data available for individual stations are shown in Table 3. It can be seen that station CHP turbine capacity ranged in size from 500MWth (No.1) to 2500MWth (No.22). The stations also have peak boilers, which usually take about half the maximum heat load, heating the network water from 110oC to 130oC. Stations 23 and 25 were still being completed in 1977. Connected loads varied from 1376MWth to 3786MWth **per station.** Some comment on the size is necessary here. Odense in Denmark, generally considered to have the largest CHP scheme in Western Europe, has a connected heat load of 925MWth. (The latest British appraisal of domestic heating, Energy Paper No. 35, considered city heat loads of around 2000MW). Thus each station has a load around the size being considered for a whole British city.

The performance of a station could be assessed on whether it meets its output targets, in terms of heat and power generation. However these are dependent on what loads the consumers present, and which stations are allocated loads, and so other efficiency indicators are used. The first indicator one might use is utilisation time for electrical capacity, and although this is normally available, for some reason it is not given in this data.

The Moscow stations produce about 70-80% of their electricity on CHP, with the exception of No 25, where the heat load was largely met by boilers, because of its state of completion. Another performance indicator is the power-to-heat ratio. Soviet figures count only the CHP electricity, whereas Swedish figures count condensing output as well. Thus Swedish figures would be expected to be higher. However, Lind provides percentages of 18-21, which compare with Moscow station figures of 30-50%, with two exceptions. These differences are striking.

Attempts to find other sources for comparison have yielded only Eastern European figures. Halzl provides 57.2, 39.2, 38.3, and 86.9 GWh/PJ (or kwh/GJ), equivalent to 21, 14, 14, and 31%, for Rumania, Poland, Hungary, and Bulgaria respectively. These figures are described as backpressure power yield of CHP turbines. Halzl suggests that figures well above 100GWh/PJ (36%) can be obtained using up-to-date power plant. The Eastern European figures relate to CHP heat only, and become 21.9, 13.6,21.9,81.5 GWh/PJ (8, 5, 8, and 29%), respectively when related to the total heat production, including heat only plants. This seems to indicate that the Moscow plant operates rather more effectively in the production of electricity, than most Swedish systems.

We have already discussed utilisation time for heat load, for the whole network. The station figures range from 2360 hrs for station No 1 to 3621 hrs for station No 22, with its industrial load. This obviously confirms the early high total network figure, compared with Swedish schemes.

From the CHP coefficient, generally 0.45-0.5, we can see that about half the heat capacity is provided by turbines, the fraction being chosen by optimisation calculations, to ensure adequate utilisation times, for expensive CHP plant. These calculations are frequently documented in the technical press, but here we can see them justified, with 80-90% of the heat provided from the turbines. Also noteworthy is that only the older inner stations retain steam supplies, except No 22 with its oil refinery load.

Looking at the fuel figures, we can see that despite statements that gas was to provide 70% of fuel by 1980, in 1977, it still had considerable way to go at 60.8%. The gas supply to power loads is interruptible in winter in favour of smaller group heating schemes. The inner city stations were still working on around one-third coal, which could not have been satisfactory from the point of view of pollution, as was evident from comments by the town-planners that these stations were now the major remaining sources of pollution in the city.

Finally we can consider the amount of fuel used for heat and power production. This is given in Soviet figures as a fuel rate based on the calorific value of a standard ton of fuel (29.3GJ/ton). The combustion heat is apportioned between heat and power giving all the CHP saving to power. Thus increased generation by CHP appears to make electricity appear more efficient, and reduces the fuel rate. The figures in Table 3 are interesting, in that they demonstrate what can happen to national efficiency figures if large amounts of electricity is generated by CHP, as Moore of the CEGB has been at pains to point out. On the other hand the figures for condensing operation are not high, reflecting the lower generating efficiency inherent in CHP plant, and possibly also the older and less efficient plant in the inner city stations. The efficiency of heat production is less problematic, and while generally over 85% does not compare with published Soviet norms of 82-88% for solid fuel, 88-92% for gas and oil.

The performance of Teploenergiya is more difficult to assess as less information is available. Table 4 shows a 6-fold capacity growth from 1961 to 1980, with load lagging behind capacity. The 1979/80 specific length is 52 m/GWh, well above that of Mosenergo, explained by the high proportion (63%) of distribution mains. The heat delivery ratio, 69 TJ/km is still higher than the Swedish range. Utilisation times have been falling since 1965 from 2750 hours to 2450 hours (1980 plan), but are also higher than the Swedish performance. The thermal efficiencies do not match this performance, particularly as they are norms and not necessarily achievements.

We may conclude from this analysis that in both these utilities, there is a high usage of plant, and a high throughput of heat to consumers. We cannot tell how efficiently the heat is then used, but Soviet newspapers frequently complain of overheating in buildings, snow melting over mains and failure to provide heat meters. A missing crucial indicator is mains losses. The figure of 6% constantly quoted can only be a norm, since the absence of meters must make losses impossible to establish by measurement. Soviet newspapers also complain about mains leaks, but these may be in the "landlords'" distribution networks, not those of the utilities.

9 ECONOMICS

All Soviet investment projects are assessed by a mechanism which combines capital and running costs and uses an 8% discount rate. Out of a number of alternative variants for a project, the preferred option has a minimum average cost Z, where $Z = C + EK$, where C is the current operating cost, E is the coefficient of relative effectiveness (usually 0.12 for the power industry, 0.15 elsewhere), and K the capital investment. This is roughly equivalent to a payback period of 8 years. However, variants are also compared for their consumption of fuel, steel, and cement, since these are some of the main material balances in the central planning.

Table 5 looks at the economics of heat supply for Mosenergo, using their own indicators. The average production cost for heat is given as 0.9625 roubles/GJ. Prices for heat, for the 1975-80 period, varied according to the medium: 1.103 roubles/GJ for hot water; 1.048-1.212 roubles/GJ for extracted steam depending on the pressure; and 1.379 roubles/GJ for live steam. Heat supplied by Mosenergo was roughly twice as expensive as that for Irkutsk (E. Siberia), (where fuel prices include much smaller transport costs), and 80% as much as Leningrad heat. The tariff was set to include a 5% profit, but is not revised regularly enough to cope with fuel price changes. Examples of power board accounting show heat sales as loss-making overall.

Under these circumstances, attempts to link wage bonuses to profits and energy conservation are likely to produce results favouring electricity rather than heat. Sales of electricity and heat are dependent on consumer demand rather than efforts by the utility. Bonuses linked to profits from sales do not therefore tend to promote energy conservation or labour productivity, as the economy needs and intends. Mosenergo is well aware of this as a problem.

According to Table 4, Teploenergiya was able to produce heat for 0.93 roubles/GJ; presumably reflecting smaller capital charges. Around 1970, it would appear heat tariffs got out of step with production costs, but that this was corrected in the next Five Year Plan.

However, the tariffs quoted are the charges to the housing "landlords", and individual consumers pay a flat rate for heating based on the size of their flat, and a per capita hot water charge. Annual charges for Moscow in 1980, were given by Ershov as 0.9 roubles/m2 of housing space (9m2/person is the usual allowance); and 7.20 roubles/person for hot water, though these are more usually quoted as monthly charges. These charges are claimed to be the result of a 50% subsidy by the state.

10 CONCLUSION

We have seen that the two Moscow utilities have moved closer together in their operation while retaining their separate finance and organisation. Mosenergo appears to restrict its operation to those of a bulk heat distributor, leaving heat load development to Teploenergiya. The utilities have high plant utilisation and throughput of heat, but are less impressive in terms of thermal efficiency, particularly since figures for mains losses are not known with any certainty. Nor can we be impressed with consumers installation which while providing their consumers with cheap heat, give no possibility or encouragement to avoid waste; though to be fair, the utilities are not to blame for this. Nevertheless this problem also occurs in heat production, where the incentive system favours electricity production at the expense of heat. Neither of these serious faults can be remedied by the utilities, but must wait for government changes.

BIBLIOGRAPHY

1. Cole, JP and German, FCA, Geography of the USSR, 2nd edition, Butterworths, London, 1970
2. Ershov, IN and Serebryanikov, NI, Teplofikatsiya Moskvy, "Energiya", Moscow, 1980
3. Halzl J, Present Status of District Heating in Eastern Europe, Fernwärme International, 1980 No 6 pp421-429
4. Hamilton FEI, The Moscow City Region, Oxford University Press, 1976.
5. Lind C-E, District Heating in Sweden, 1972-77, Energy Policy 1979 March pp74-76.
6. Lipenskii GV, Moskovskaya energeticheskaya, Moscow 1976.
7. Moore AG and Nixon KA, Thermal efficiencies of electicity systems in EEC countries, Journal of the Institute of Energy, June 1981 pp103-112.
8. Segedinov AA, Inzhenernye kommunikatsii v ekonomike gradostroitel´stva, Stroiizdat, Moscow, 1968.
9. Steklov V Yu, Razvitie elektro-energeticheskogo khozyaistva SSSR, Energiya, Moscow, 1979
10. Thörnqvist L, Efficiency Differences in District Heating Systems, IV International District Heating Conference Brescia, Italy 1980, Section 2-14.

Table 1   Development of Moscow´s CHP network

		1945	1960	1975	1981[3]
Electrical cap.	MW	204	1000	5068	
Heating cap.	MW	872	5060	22100	27000
Connected heat load	MW	617	4560	20800	
No. of stations		5(1940)[1]	10(1964)[2]	14(1977)	13
Length of mains	km	90	645	2155	2720
Output of elec.	Gwh	1000	5040	24499	
Output of heat	mill.GJ	6.70	50.66	202.23	280

Source: Ershov 1980: p44 except 1. Ershov 1980: p82
                                   2. NDHA 1967: p12
                                   3. Lipovskikh 1982: p81

Table 2   Network and plant efficiency

	1945	1960	1975	1981
Specific length* m/GWh	48.36	45.83	38.36	34.97
Heat delivery ratio TJ/km	74.4	78.5	93.84	102.9
Utilisation time hrs	3016	3086	2700	

*   specific length = mains length/output of heat, m/GWh
heat delivery ratio = heat output/mains length, TJ/km
    utilisation time = heat output/connected load hrs

Source: calculated from Table 1.

Table 3   Main Moscow CHP stations in 1977

	Station No										Total for all
	1	9	11	12	16	20	21	22	23	25	
Electrical output GWh	617	2423	1593	1922	2072	4214	6853	7210	5588	428	32920
% of elec. by CHP	99.9	79.0	72.5	75.5	78.3	72.9	76.0	65.0	69.5	24.5	72.1
Unit elec.output by CHP kwh/GJ**	64.7	90.8	85.0	72.8	106.5	129.7	140.0	123.7	150.0	83.7	115.8
(%)	23	33	31	26	38	47	50	45	54	30	41
Av. connected heat load MW	1376	2018	1721	2253	1818	2815	3736	3408	2571	441	2215/
Turbine heat cap MW	500	1179	816	1064	811	1372	1884	2493	1512	322	11952
CHP coefficient*	0.36	0.58	0.47	0.47	0.45	0.49	0.50	0.73	0.59	——	0.54
Heat output TJ	11688	22890	16957	23962	17456	26805	43779	44420	30544	4568	243072
% in hot water	99.1	60.0	80.7	75.8	99.9	99.9	99.8	87.7	99.8	100.0	90.1
Heat from CHP %	81.4	92.1	80.2	83.0	87.2	88.4	85.1	85.3	84.7	27.5	84.2
Heat from peak boilers %	17.7	5.0	6.7	11.6	9.7	9.8	14.7	8.7	15.1	72.5	12.0
Fuel supply % gas	86.0	64.8	62.0	62.5	69.6	76.9	43.0	35.4	49.3	100.0	60.8
% oil	14.0	35.2	1.0	3.6	4.3	6.0	57.0	5.7	50.7	——	26.2
% coal	0.0	0.0	37.0	33.9	26.1	27.1	0.0	69.9	0.0	——	13.0
Fuel usage rate g/kwh	149.6	211.1	243.3	224.8	226.0	226.3	207.1	248.0	220.4	365.1	225.9
Efficiency %	82.1	58.2	50.5	54.7	54.4	54.3	59.3	49.5	55.7	33.7	54.4
Fuel usage on condensing g/kwh	——	416.5	468.9	432.8	466.8	415.6	372.7	412.5	364.6	——	404.0
Efficiency %		29.5	26.2	28.4	26.3	30.0	33.0	29.8	33.7	——	30.4
Fuel usage for heat prodn kg/GJ	38.5	39.7	40.0	40.1	40.0	40.2	40.2	41.3	40.6	38.6	40.3
Efficiency %	88.6	86.0	85.3	85.1	85.3	84.9	84.9	82.6	84.1	88.4	84.7
Utilisation time hrs	2360	3150	2736	2954	2666	2644	3255	3621	3300	2871	3047

Source: Ershov 1980: p72

NOTES

* CHP coefficient = $\dfrac{\text{Turbine heat capacity}}{\text{Turbine heat cap. + Hot water boiler cap.}}$

** Unit electrical output = $\dfrac{\text{electrical output by CHP}}{\text{heat output from CHP}}$

Table 4 Performance indicators for **Teploenergiya**

		1961	1965	1970	1975	1980(plan)
Boilerhouse installed capacity	MW	1025	3220	3880	5746	6821
Heat load	MW	582	1970	2840	4350	5704
Heat output	mill.GJ	2.2	19.5	27.3	38.1	50.3
Fuel usage norm	kg/GJ	47.3	41.2	40.4	40.4	40.4
Efficiency	%	72.2	82.8	84.5	84.5	84.5
Production cost	roub/GJ	1.04	0.75	0.92	0.90	0.93
Tariff	roub/GJ	0.98	0.84	0.89	0.94	0.95
Labour productivity	manhrs/GJ	0.73	0.18	0.13	0.11	0.10
Utilisation time	hrs	1050	2750	2670	2432	2450

Source: Ershov 1980: p161

Table 5 Economic indicators for Moscow CHP stations and other stations in 1977

	Moscow CHP stations	Mosenergo thermal stations	Minenergo USSR thermal stations
Average fuel price rub/ton			
for electricity output	18.36	19.28	15.48
for heat output	18.47	18.37	15.72
Unit cost of electrical capacity rub/kw	155.4	152.1	145.8
Annual use of installed			
electrical capacity hrs	5985	5623	5737
Own power consumption			
electricity %	4.05	4.79	4.92
heat kwh/GJ	8.27	8.07	7.31
Fuel usage			
electricity output g/kwh	225.8	279.0	334.4
heat output kg/GJ	40.3	40.47	41.37
Production cost structure			
electricity kop / 10 kwh	5.58	7.31	6.68
fuel %	74.4	71.8*	66.0
fixed costs %	8.4	9.3*	12.3
depreciation %	17.2	18.5*	21.7
heat roub / 10 GJ	0.9625	0.979	0.928
fuel %	77.3	75.9	69.8
fixed costs %	8.0	8.8	11.7
depreciation %	14.7	15.2	18.5

*percentages total 99.6 because data given in source does not total 7.31

Source: Ershov 1980: p46

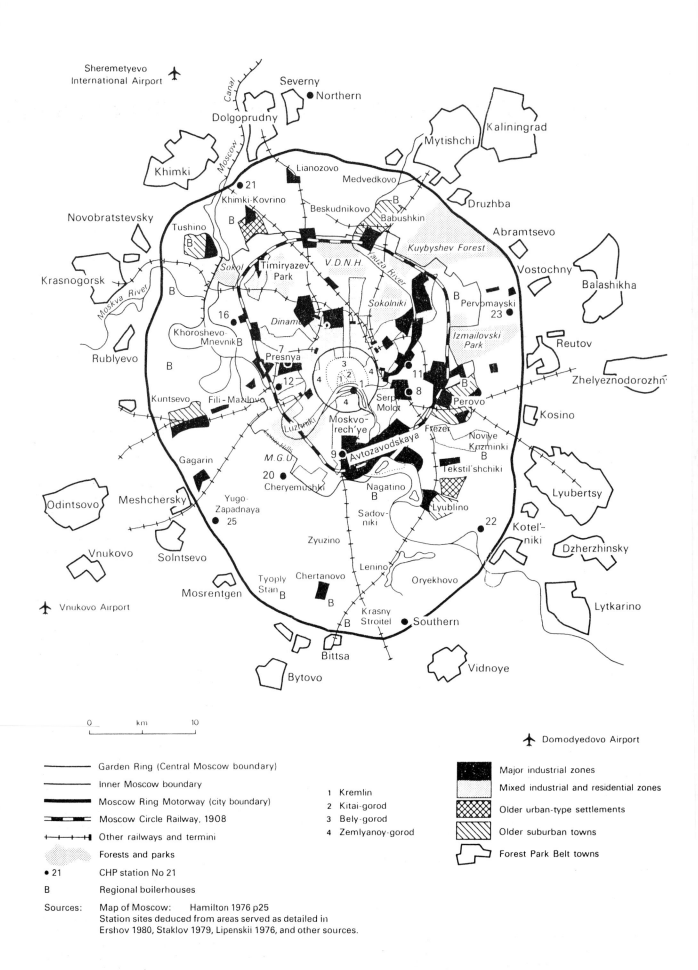

Sheremetyevo International Airport ✈

Severny
● Northern

Dolgoprudny

Kaliningrad

Mytishchi

Khimki

Druzhba

Lianozovo
Medvedkovo

● 21
Khimki-Kovrino
B

Novobratstevsky
Beskudnikovo
B
Babushkin

Abramtsevo

Tushino
B

Vostochny

Kuybyshev Forest

Krasnogorsk
Sokol
Timiryazev Park
V.D.N.H.
Balashikha

Moskva River
B

Sokolniki
B
Pervomayski
23 ●

Reutov

16
Dinamo
Izmailovski Park

Rublyevo
Khoroshevo-Mnevnik B
7
Presnya
Zhelyeznodorozhn

B
11
B

Kuntsevo
Fili-Maxlovo
12
4
1
8
Perovo

Kosino

Luzhniki
Serp Molot
Frezer
Noviye Kuzminki
B

Gagarin
M.G.U
9
Avtozavodskaya
Tekstil'shchiki

Lyubertsy

Meshchersky
20 ●
Cheryemushki
Nagatino
B
Lyublino

Odintsovo

Yugo-Zapadnaya
25 ●
Sadov-niki

22 ●
Kotel'-niki

Dzherzhinsky

Vnukovo
Solntsevo
Zyuzino
Lenino
Oryekhovo

Lytkarino

✈ Vnukovo Airport
Tyoply Stan B
Chertanovo
B

Mosrentgen
Krasny Stroitel
B
Southern

Vidnoye

B
Bittsa

Bytovo

0   km   10

✈ Domodyedovo Airport

——————— Garden Ring (Central Moscow boundary)

——————— Inner Moscow boundary

━━━━━━━ Moscow Ring Motorway (city boundary)

━┅━┅━ Moscow Circle Railway, 1908

+┼+┼+┼+ Other railways and termini

▓▓▓ Forests and parks

● 21   CHP station No 21

B   Regional boilerhouses

1 Kremlin
2 Kitai-gorod
3 Bely-gorod
4 Zemlyanoy-gorod

█ Major industrial zones

░ Mixed industrial and residential zones

▨ Older urban-type settlements

▨ Older suburban towns

⬡ Forest Park Belt towns

Sources: Map of Moscow: Hamilton 1976 p25
           Station sites deduced from areas served as detailed in
           Ershov 1980, Staklov 1979, Lipenskii 1976, and other sources.

Fig 1   Moscow CHP and district heating stations

Co-generation in the field of public utilities supply

F T F WIGGIN, DFH, CEng, FIEE, FINucE

SYNOPSIS The paper discusses the practical outcome of technical and economic decisions taken on investment in co-generation plant during the ten years 1975-85 against the background of some 60 years of CHP utilities supply operations by Slough Estates plc at their Slough Trading Estate. Fuel prices and tariff applications related to the requirement for a competitive economic end result from co-generation undertakings in the utilities supply field are discussed in some detail. Comment is also made regarding the effect of these factors on technical decisions concerning co-generation plant dispositions at Slough and in the United Kingdom compared to that in other countries. The paper postulates the likely future scenario for the development of co-generation in the United Kingdom during the next 15 years based on the discussions of the experience to date.

1 INTRODUCTION

The technical and economic impact of co-generation in the field of public utilities supply can be discussed by reviewing the background, outcome and future of both conventional and CHP operations within a single undertaking. Slough Estates plc has been concerned in overall utilities operations for some 60 years involving the supply of electricity, steam, water and gas to public consumers in the industrial, commercial and domestic sectors of the marketplace. These consumers are mainly the valued tenants of the Company's industrial or commercial properties on trading estates at Slough and Birmingham, but approximately 2000 domestic consumers as well as some other industrial/commercial local demands which are not related to tenancies are supplied adjacent to the Slough Industrial Estate on the basis of historical undertaking. Under the provisions of the Slough Trading Company Act 1925 the utilities undertaking concerned in operations at Slough supplies annually over 200 million units of electricity and over 190 million kilogrammes of steam to some 800 factories occupied by over 300 companies employing some 25,000 persons in over 6.3 million square metres of manufacturing, warehousing and commercial accommodation from its power station base of CHP generation. The installed electrical and main boiler steam raising capacities are some 90 megawatts and 400,000 Kg/hour respectively but the station also annually pumps supplies of some 5000 million litres of potable water to some 800 premises from the Company's own wells and reservoirs. Gas and heavy residual oil are the fuels burned by both the boilers and recently installed extremely efficient Gas Turbine/fired Heat Recovery Boiler combined unit since coal burning was discontinued in the late 1960s

for the requirements of development space and environmental reasons. Steam and Electricity generation involved in the supply of heat and power to consumers can be separated into two spheres of operation for comparative purposes. Fig.1 shows the schematic layout of the main plant used in the production and supply of steam and electricity over the past ten years. Fig.2 indicates this overall system separated into the CHP sphere with new combined cycle co-generation (shown under A) and the conventional sphere of operations (shown under B). These 'in house' facilities are supplemented by a third sector which involves the use of the grid interconnection for the import of electrical energy (shown under C). It will be appreciated that, since the overall system and requirements of operation at Slough are complex, some simplification of these systems has been assumed for the purposes of technical and economic discussion.

2 FUEL CONSIDERATIONS

No consideration of these three sectors would be valid without noting the main basis of their individual and combined economics. During the past ten years of consideration, generation operations at Slough have been based on oil and natural gas fuels only. The reintroduction of coal and the burning of solid wastes have been seriously considered during this time, but, for reasons of space and environment resulting from an 'Inner City' type location of both the Company's Power Station and the Trading Estate, no investment in these fuels has been made. This situation has resulted in the economics of comparative operations moving in favour of increasing the use of the grid interconnector since the nationalised sector of electricity generation is based preponderantly on coal burning.

TABLE 1

COMPARISON IN PENCE/THERM OF INPUT FUEL/ENERGY FOR UTILITIES OPERATIONS

Year	Average Price for Coal	Average Price For Residual HFO	Average Price for GAS (Interruptable)	SLOUGH ESTATES Aggregate Price for Input FUEL/ENERGY PURCHASES	NATIONALISED SECTOR Aggregate Price for Input FUEL/ENERGY PURCHASES
1976	7.9	13.0	10.0	7.6	8.0
1977	8.8	16.4	12.6	8.9	9.0
1978	9.7	14.3	14.4	11.7	10.2
1979	11.0	15.8	15.9	14.7	11.7
1980	13.8	25.2	18.7	19.5	14.2
1981	17.0	29.0	23.0	23.9	17.4
1982	17.7	31.0	24.8	24.9	18.0
1983	18.5	31.6	25.0	25.2	18.6
1984	19.0	47.0	27.0	27.9 – 27.3*	27.2 – 18.9*
1985	19.9	43.0	28.9	29.2	Est.20.0

* Adjusted to omit estimated effects of miners' strike.

TABLE 2

COMPARISON OF NATIONALISED SECTOR/SLOUGH ESTATES THERMAL EFFICIENCIES

Year	Nationalised Sector Av. System % (Fossil Fired)	Slough Estates Av. % (S.O.)	Difference as %
1976	31.6	36.3	+ 12.9
1977	31.5	37.6	+ 16.2
1978	31.8	38.8	+ 18.0
1979	31.7	39.3	+ 19.3
1980	32.2	37.7	+ 14.6
1981	33.8	38.6	+ 12.4
1982	34.1	41.0	+ 16.8
1983	34.3	39.7	+ 13.6
1984	34.3	38.7	+ 11.3
1985	34.5 Est.	38.4	+ 10.2

Table 1 shows the average prices of oil, gas and coal for utilities operations over the last decade. These clearly indicate the disparity in fuel costs arising from the use of these fossil based fuels. Fig. 3 shows the overall comparative price outcome in graphic form and emphasises the adverse cost effect on Slough Estates compared to the nationalised sector's mainly coal based generation.

3 COMBINED HEAT & POWER OPERATIONS (PRIOR TO 1983)

Prior to 1983 when the new co-generation plant began commercial operations, steam was generated at 4309 kPa 440°c utilising boilers capable of both natural gas and residual oil firing. This steam was used for electricity generation by utilising turbo alternators with input steam conditions of 4137 kPa 440°c and pass out facilities at 1379 kPa 316°c for the distribution of steam heat to consumers. Fig. 4 shows in graphic form the average range of thermal efficiencies applying to

this type of operation during the period of review. For the purposes of indicating the relationship of CHP thermal efficiencies to the electricity/steam heat energy balance a plot of the ratio: Electrical Energy Sales plus Steam energy sales divided by Electrical Energy Sales is also shown over the same period. Fig.5 shows in graphic form the relationship of thermal efficiency and this energy balance ratio for CHP operations with and without combined cycle addition.

4 CONVENTIONAL OPERATIONS

The term conventional operations in this context covers the generation of electricity at Slough by raising steam at 4309 kPa 440°c with boilers fired by natural gas or residual oil and utilising condensing only turbo alternators of various manufacture. Fig. 4 includes in graphic form a plot of the average range of thermal efficiencies applying to this type of electricity generation as a comparison with the efficiences of CHP operations.

5 GRID INTERCONNECTION

The Grid interconnection capacity at Slough has only been capable of supplying between 25% and 35% of the total consumer demand depending on seasonal factors. Prior to the introduction of the Energy Act 1983 the grid interconnection was mainly used for the import of electricity on an incremental cost basis of comparison with 'in house' generation. Some mutual benefit of load management was also obtained during the winter periods under the appropriate nationalised sector tariffs applying at the time. Table 2 shows a comparison of the average annual overall thermal efficiencies of generation for the nationalised sector and Slough Estates for the period of review.

6 THE IMPACT OF COMBINED CYCLE CO-GENERATION

The combined effect during the late 1970s of the widening adverse disparity in fuel prices (see Table 1) and reducing favourable margin of overall thermal efficiency (See Table 2) required remedial action by Slough Estates. It was decided to invest in a gas turbine co-generation plant which could be operated in combined cycle within the existing CHP operations.

This plant is capable of sustained commercial operations using either or both natural gas or residual oil as a fuel in both the gas turbine and the fired heat recovery boiler. The Gas Turbine/alternator provides some 22 Mw (at 11kV) of electricity generation capacity and the fired Heat Recovery Boiler some 12.6 Kg/S (4309 kPa 440°c) in waste heat mode rising to 25Kg/S in augmented firing mode with duct burners in use. The turn down flexibility and performance of the plant is exceptional and continuous operation with 12Mw of electricity generation and 6Kg/S of steam supply is a regular occurrence.

The existing pass out turbo alternators used for CHP operations under (A) have been refurbished and are used for backend electricity generation in the combined cycle using steam supplied by the fired heat recovery boiler. Commercial operations of the unit has had considerable technical impact as denoted by the fact that this mode now provides some 60% of the total Slough Estates generation. The availability of the new Gas Turbine/fired Heat Recovery Boilerplant has averaged some 88% for the period 1st January 1985 to 1st January 1986 with a utilisation factor of some 83% over the same period. During this period the Gas Turbine has operated on residual oil fuel for some 440 hours due to the interruption of gas fuel supplies. The cost of residual oil treatment can be noted as adding approximately 5-6% to the delivered price of the fuel as averaged and shown in Table 1.

An indication of the economic impact of this co-generation operation can be seen in Fig. 4 which shows the average range of the thermal efficiencies being achieved since 1980 as an extension of those achieved by CHP operations prior to installation of the new plant. This is particularly the case when the graph of overall thermal efficiently corrected for movements in the

TABLE 3

COMPARISON COST OF UNITS TRANSFERRED FOR DISTRIBUTION

Annual Period	CEGB p/kWh Sold	Slough Estates p/kWh Transferred	% Difference
1976-1977	1.51	1.50	+
1980-1981	2.64	4.38	- 29.73
1983-1984	3.26	4.00	- 18.50
1984-1985	4.34	4.22	+ 2.84

TABLE 4

COMBINED CYCLE COMPARISON COST OF UNITS TRANSFERRED FOR DISTRIBUTION

Annual Period	CEGB p/kWh Sold	Slough Estates p/kWh Transferred	Slough Estates Combined Cycle Only p/kWh Transferred
1976-1977	1.51	1.50	-
1980-1981	2.64	4.38	-
1983-1984	3.26	4.00	3.24
1984-1985	4.34	4.22	3.36

balance of electricity and steam demands is taken into account. The improvement in the thermal efficiency of electricity only generation resulting from Gas Turbine operations is also emphatic.

Perhaps the best way of discussing the technical and economic impact of such operations is to compare the average overall sent out cost of electricity production in terms of a unit sold by the CEGB and a unit supplied and transferred by Slough Estates generation over the period of review. Table 3 is self explanatory in terms of impact since the figures include operating costs on a comparable basis of accounting. This is particularly the case when the adverse disparity of some 31.5% in fuel costs as compared to the CEGB's aggregate fuel/energy input (See Table 1) and the necessity to meet consumer steam heat requirements at Slough are taken into account.

It will be appreciated that Table 3 shows the cost of electricity supplied from total Slough Estates generation operations. The economic impact of the new combined cycle operation within this base of undertaking is much more evident if the cost of transfer from this mode of operation only is identified for comparison purposes. Table 4 shows clearly the competiveness of combined cycle operations in spite of the adverse differential fuel or energy input costs indicated in Table 1. In this regard, it should be noted that the operating thermal efficiency of the Combined Cycle output (within the overall operational situation) has averaged 65.7%, 68.0% and 66.2% for the years 1983-84-85 respectively as a result of operations within the Electricity/Steam Energy Balance Ratio range of 2.9 to 3.1.

7 FUTURE DISPOSITIONS

The economic competitiveness of this combined cycle operation has done much to restore the adverse economic consequences arising from the previously noted trend of increasing disparity in fuel costs and erosion of the margin of thermal efficiency required to compete with the nationalised sector. However, this favourable effect has been drastically reduced by the increasing high cost of continuing 'in house' conventional generation (see Fig. 4 after 1981). Accordingly, an investment decision has been taken to increase the capacity of grid interconnection with a view to dispensing with all the conventional generation at Slough for the medium term. This revised operational regime will be established by 1987 when only the combined cycle co-generation plant will be operated in parallel with the reinforced grid connection. The latter will provide a coal based generation electricity supply input to the Slough Estates undertaking.

On the basis of present analysis and forecast, it is anticipated that the combined cycle regime for electricity and steam supplies to consumers at Slough will remain competitive for most of this decade compared with the alternative of total electrical import and boiler only steam supply operations. However, the overall economic outcome of the utilities undertaking at Slough remains enigmatic since the field of public utilities continues to be subjected to the short term vagaries of political and fiscal expediency. This combined with rapid changes in international exchange rates and fuel availability emphasises the difficulties of forecasting the economic outcome of utilities operations.

8 TARIFF CONSIDERATIONS

The background provided by the figures for fuel prices, thermal efficiencies of operation and energy balance of supply clearly indicate that, whilst the base of combined cycle operations is competitive in terms of both a comparison with the nationalised sector and in economic outcome, conventional operations can only continue to operate at a loss. Since the Company's tariffs for electricity steam and water on the Slough Estate have to compete with those applying in surrounding locations, the tariffs related to producing income revenue for the Utilities undertaking equate with those issued by the nationalised sector for electricity and water. The tariff for steam heat is fixed within the balance of requirement to recover all related operating costs with an element of profit and the constraint of a pricing requirement to ensure that the tenant consumers concerned will find it in their interest to neither proceed to install their own steam raising plant nor use an alternative form of heat energy. It has been found from experience that tenant consumers are unlikely to consider installing their own steam raising plant provided the price of steam supplied to them is within the range ± 10% as compared to either generating it themselves or considering alternatives.

In this context, it is pertinent to note that the Slough Estates tariff for steam heat has of necessity to relate to the price of their gas and oil fuel inputs and therefore a tenant consumer prepared to use coal for steam raising should obtain a cheaper outcome. However, it has been found in practice that the downside of risks involved in embarking on 'in house' steam raising facilities continues to be a deterrent in this context, particularly for the small to medium type of consumer. The reliability of the Slough Estates Utilities undertaking has also contributed to the reluctance of tenant consumers to consider alternative energy forms and even in the field of space heating, where the tariff on offer is at a disadvantage when compared to direct gas fired installation, a growth of consumption is still evident. However, it must be noted that the serious decline of the British manufacturing industry during the last ten years has had a very adverse affect on the steam/electricity generation balance for efficient CHP operations.

Short of investing in coal burning operations, the only viable alternative to the present inefficient conventional operations is to import electricity from the grid and maximise export to the local network at times of mutual advantage. Therefore, the tariffs on offer for these purposes from the nationalised sector are of vital economic concern to Slough. Unfortunately, the co-ordination of the import/export requirements for parallel operations in terms of nationalised sector tariff provisions leaves much to be desired as instanced by the anomaly of conflicting shoulder month demand and unit charge applications during the 1985/86 winter period within the purchase and export tariffs quoted to Slough Estates. The Energy Act 1983 has done little to resolve this difficulty since it stems from natural attitudes relating to the actual structure of the Electricity Supply Industry within the U.K. but particularly in England and Wales.

9 ECONOMIC RELATIONSHIPS OF OPERATIONAL FACTORS

The complexity of CHP operations at Slough requires some form of simplified model for an understanding of the relationship between the various major operational factors which affect economic viability of the undertaking as a whole. Figure 6 represents a reasonable attempt to provide such a model. This model shows the relationship between the three most important factors. These are the overall thermal efficiency of operation, the CHP Energy Balance Ratio of demand and the differential fuel cost between Slough Estates and the nationalised sector since the latter in effect set the price level of electricity sold or imported. Outcome economic viability as a target for the model can be noted as being payment of all interest and depreciation charges over 20 years with a 10% annual return on capital invested. With some reservations arising from a very complex situation, the graph shown establishes the relationship necessary to achieve target economic viability at Slough within the parameters of existing operations.

An explanation of the model can be obtained by noting as an example that Point A represents the overall average station thermal efficiency for the 1984/85 period say 38.5%. The related CHP Energy Balance Ratio over the same timescale amounts to approximately 1.75 for this technical efficiency. Reading across to the scale for percentage differential fuel cost in favour of the nationalised sector it can be noted that this operational mode relating to Point A would require a fuel differential not exceeding some 6.0% (in favour of the nationalised sector) for economic viabilityto be achieved. Similarly, Point B represents the Overall average of strict Combined cycle thermal efficiency of say

66.0% for this type of operation during 1984/85 and relates to an Energy Balance Ratio for it of some 3.0. Again reading across to the fuel differential scale it can be seen that an adverse fuel cost of approximately 33.0% in favour of the nationalised sector can be sustained assuming this was the only operational mode used. These examples reflect the position of sold or transferred costs noted in Table 4. This model obviously permits a facility for establishing the limits of any two of the other factors given initial assumption in respect of one of the three defined as being relevant to a test for economic viability. It would be interesting to check the outcome and relationship of existing or postulated CHP schemes using this model for locations other than at Slough.

The model clearly shows the impact of co-generation operations as compared to conventional generation in the utilities field of supply taking into account the major factors which determine economic outcome at Slough. Whilst it must be emphasised that the combined cycle operation cannot actually be separated from the existing complex mix of generation without considering the complications of overhead cost transfers, the margin in hand on the fuel cost differential is obviously such as to underwrite the profitability of a similar undertaking in a greenfield situation. This is particularly the case if average operating overall co-generation thermal efficiencies of the order of 55 plus %, related to Energy Balance ratios in excess of 2.5 can be obtained using coal as a fuel since the latter would give a virtual zero differential compared to the nationalised sector. A recent study has indicated that an investment of the order of £180/kW installed (Electrical plus Thermal Heat equivalent) would be required for a coal burning co-generation plant suitable for this purpose in the Slough situation. A further investment in both steam and electricity distribution would obviously be necessary for a 'greenfield' site installation.

10 COMMENT

The experience at Slough, including the decade of years covered in some detail by this paper, establishes that co-generation provides an appropriate base for dealing with the complex requirements of electricity, steam and water supply to the public in general and industry in particular. A successful tender for local district heating supplies in the mid-70s at Slough confirmed that the heating requirements of low density domestic housing can be met from an industrial CHP centre of operation with a satisfactory economic outcome notwithstanding the absence of space heating demand in the summer. The fact thatthe scheme was abandoned as a result of housing policy changes arising from local elections only confirms that the attitudes arising from the organisation of this country are the predominant factor which prevents the future development of combined heat and power in the United Kingdom. The problems resulting from the evolvement of our particular kind of social organisation and governmental procedure ensure a positive resistance to change which takes little account of any outcome benefit which cannot be realised within a short timescale of less than five years.

This situation particularly operates against changes of any significance in the field of utilities undertaking since the adoption of a longer term view is essential. This is necessary for the obvious reason that the conceptual project lead in time (involving research, design, planning permission, various inspectorate and governmental clearances, construction followed by commissioning) when added to the timescale required for adequate payback on a heavy investment commitment ensures that a long term consideration must predominate. Since virtually all the organisational and working institutions of the United Kingdom have been historically founded and continue to function on the basis of a system which adopts a confrontational approach to virtually all procedures, including industrial relations, it cannot be surprising that an extreme view is encouraged from both opponents and supporters of any venture which seeks to significantly change the 'status quo'. The long standing debate on the future of CHP/co-generation in the United Kingdom is just one example of this position. The self evident fact of the success of this type of undertaking on the Continent and elsewhere in the world is unlikely, therefore, to affect developments here until the nationalised sector of public electricity supply positively supports co-generation within its own activities as a matter of direct self interest.

This self interest is at present invested in large 'centralised' power stations located for convenience of fuel supply, cooling water availability and ash disposal since the grid system gives considerable flexibility in terms of any requirement for close proximity to industrial or urban load centres. The attitudes engendered by this type of operational disposition quite naturally underwrite the existing position since the introduction of any major change in direction would certainly be uncomfortable. The fact that the Electricity Supply Industry has an over capacity of generating plant at present must support a defensive stance which takes the view that any change or innovation which requires major investment in new plant should be resisted. This situation is understandable and indeed Slough Utilities have had to deal with their own problems against a similar background, albeit the resistance to change centres on continuing the existing CHP operations against the background of an overcapacity in conventional generation. However, Slough Estates have taken the overall view that investment in effective techniques which seek a significant increase in efficiency with satisfactory economic outcome should be pursued irrespective of the discomfort and risks resulting from the changes introduced. The recent installation of the Combined Cycle Co-generation plant within the existing CHP operation is the first phase of a policy arising from this view.

Against this background, the development of co-generation within the nationalised sphere of electricity supply is likely to follow the path of a tentative probing in the direction of improving the efficiency of auxiliary operations as an adjunct to the main 'centralised' type of conventional generation. Peripheral involvement in certain research activities e.g. in fluidised bed and coal gasification experiments by the nationalised sector, will shortly be reinforced by major developments outside the United Kingdom which could result in a slow change of attitude towards the introduction of co-generation into the field of public electricity supply. It is postulated that this will not result from any commitment to CHP operations but from the fact that techniques are now emerging which will increase the thermal efficiency of 'centralised' electricity generation within the next decade from the present ceiling level of under 40% up to 50% and beyond using coal as fuel. Some of these developments can be exampled by directing attention to the papers given at the International Congress on Combustion Engines in Oslo during June 1985 and mentioning the Cool Water Coal Gasification Combined Cycle Plant program in California and the Kiln Gas system development in Illinois, the projected development by Brown Boveri of the British Gas/Lurgi system, the ASEA/Stal replanting of the Vartan (CHP) Power Station in Sweden using Pressurised Fluidised Bed technique for combined cycle co-generation, etc. These coal fuel based developments for combined cycle co-generation applications can shortly be associated with single shaft unit sizes of between 500 and 1000 MW capacity including advanced reheat possibilities. Large multi shaft and single shaft Gas Turbine/Steam Turbine combinations are already being installed and commissioned in Tohoku, Kyushu, Chubu and Tokyo in Japan. This progress opens up the prospect of co-generation on a scale close to the ideal espoused for large power station generation in the United Kingdom. The medium term scenario for cogeneration operations therefore appears to be that of a coal fuel based first stage, of either a pressure fluidised bed or coal gasification process, with a second stage involving a gas turbine or other prime mover (with direct electricity generation) followed by heat recovery for a third stage of steam turbine electricity generation, with or without passout or back pressure for steam heat supply to consumers, depending on the future development of CHP schemes in this country. Experience in Germany, Austria and Japan has already confirmed that 'centralised' operations on a scale using 200-500 MW Gas Turbines for co-generation lends itself to the development of the above scenario by the introduction of a coal fuel based first stage as an input to large industrial gas turbines. It should be understood, however, that this technology requires a utility undertaking which crosses the present boundaries of demarcation between the Coal Board, the nationalised Electricity Supply Industry and British Gas Corporation. Accordingly, the factor of our organisation and associated confrontational system of procedure can once again be expected to delay the benefits of exploiting these advances. Unfortunately, the scale of such operations is such as to preclude Slough Estates from obtaining the full benefit of the gains now possible from these developments but the ASEA-Stal project in Sweden is being watched with interest since this does have the possiblity of a small scale application.

11 CONCLUSION

The Slough Estates Utilities undertaking is a complex operation involving both CHP and conventional modes of operation. The success of the undertaking over some 60 years has been underwritten by a willingness of the Company to be flexible in the face of changes over the entire range of the factors which affect the economic viability of its Utilities Services Division. This paper covers the major investment decisions taken during the past decade to 1985 as a response to such changes. Almost without exception, these changes have been economically against continuing the mix of simple CHP and conventional type operations as conducted in the previous decade to 1975. The main conclusion to be drawn from the facts and figures provided is that without the recent investment in a combined cycle addition, using very advanced co-generation techniques, the electricity generating activities would have ceased at Slough for obvious economic reasons.

The impact of this co-generation addition is clearly demonstrated within the relationships shown in Table 4 and the model in Fig.6 which compares the Point A (existing mix of operations) and Point B (combined cycle operations using co-generation) operational modes. The present adverse fuel differential of some 31.5% in favour of the nationalised sector can only be tolerated in the medium term because of the high thermal efficiency and good economics resulting from the combined cycle operation inherent in the Point B situation. However, the reduction of this adverse fuel differential in conjunction with the optimisation of existing operations are the objectives being most vigorously pursued and an investment in reinforcing the grid interconnection with the nationalised sector is one action to that end.

The Fig. 6 model also shows the extent to which major factors which affect the economic viability of CHP schemes in general can be varied within the constraint of a satisfactory overall outcome. It should be noted that the use of a co-generation combined cycle operation enhances the overall thermal efficiency of the undertaking to such an extent that non-coal burning operations can be considered as being economically satisfactory within the constraints of relationship shown in the model.

12 REFERENCES

(1) All statistics for the nationalised sector have been extracted from the relevant Annual Report and Accounts for the Electricity Council and the Central Electricity Generating Board.

(2) PLUMLEY, D.R. Combined Cycle Power from Coal, CIMAC International Congress Oslo T31 (June 1985)

(3) KEHLHOFER, R. Combined Cycle 300MW with Coal Gasification, CIMAC International Congress Oslo T43 (June 1985)

(4) ARAKI, R. Operating Experience of MW701D Gas Turbine Burning LNG in a Combined Cycle Plant, CIMAC International Congress Oslo T20 (June 1985)

STEAM SYSTEM

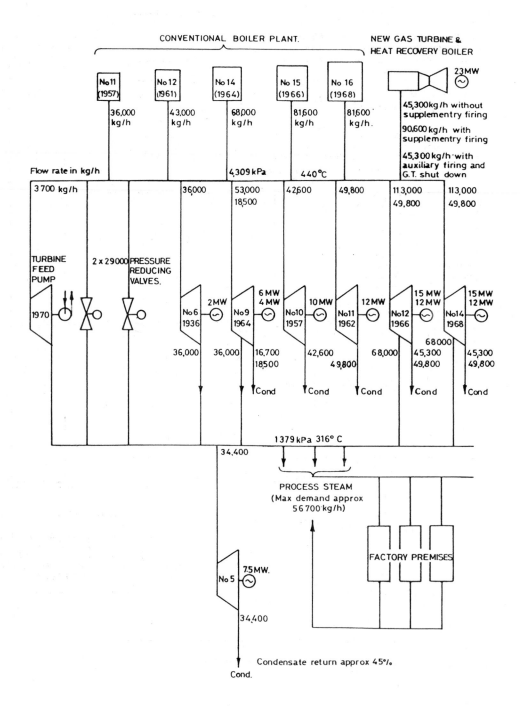

Fig 1

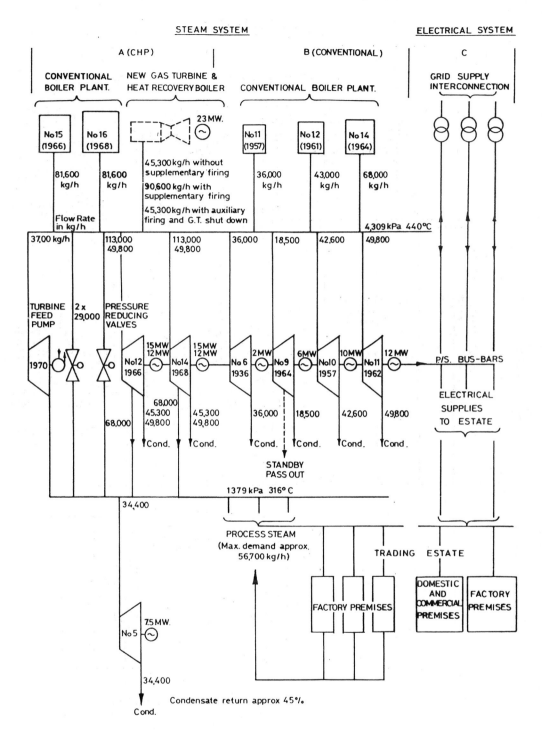

Fig 2

COMPARISON OF INPUT ENERGY COSTS

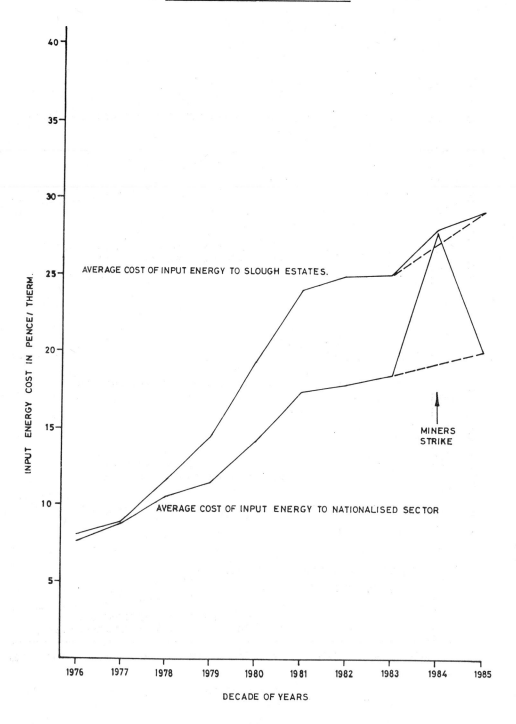

Fig 3

COMPARISON OF THERMAL EFFICIENCES.

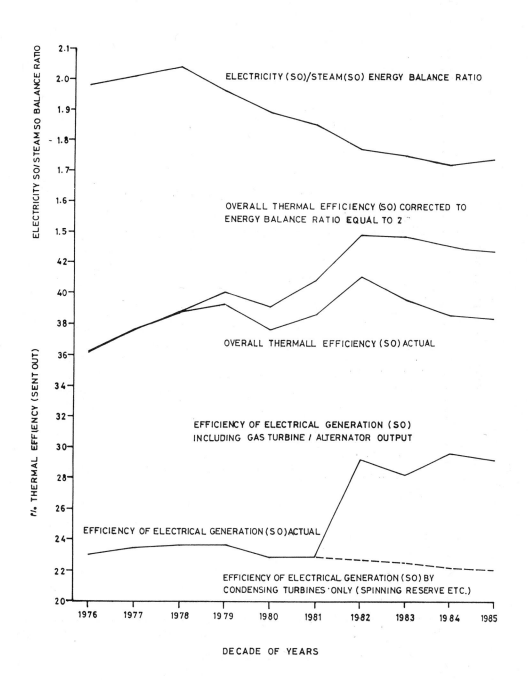

Fig 4

EFFECT OF ELECTRICITY / STEAM ENERGY BALANCE
ON THERMAL EFFICIENCY

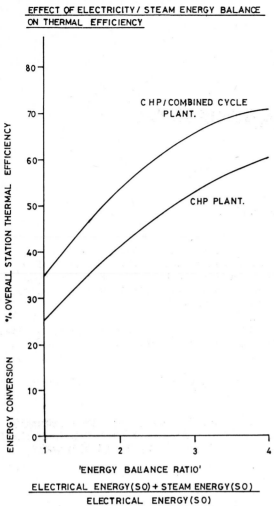

Fig 5

MODEL FOR RELATIONSHIP OF FUEL COST DIFFERENTIAL/THERMAL EFFICIENCY/ENERGY BALANCE RATIO

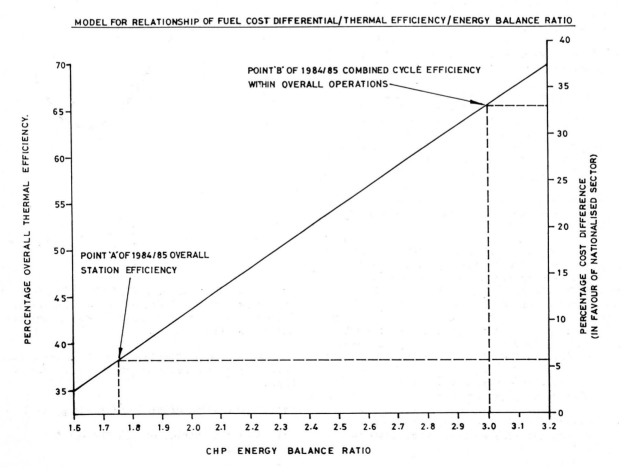

Fig 6

34

The Shell experience in co-generation

B W GAINEY, BSc, PhD, FRSC
Shell International Petroleum Co.Ltd, London
P A WARD, MA
Shell UK Oil Ltd, London
(Formerly Director, Shell Industrial Energy Management, Rotterdam, Holland)

SYNOPSIS   In 1980/81 a study undertaken for the Dutch Government concluded that a valuable cogeneration market existed in the Netherlands but that two critical factors were the lack of financing and a reluctance of many companies to work with unfamiliar technology. Building upon previous experience with cogeneration projects a Netherlands subsidiary, Shell Industrial Energy Management (SIEM) was started to explore this niche in the energy market.

SIEM offers a complete energy management service to industrial clients including system design, equipment procurement, installation, optimisation, operation, maintenance and finance. Contracts with the client are normally for ten years.

This paper briefly reviews the Dutch market for cogeneration, possible financing schemes and Shell's experience and projects in this new, novel business arena.

1   INTRODUCTION

Recently in several countries there has been a resurgence in the use of combined heat and power (CHP) in the industrial sector.

This reverses a trend (see Figure 1) over the last twenty-five years that saw the share of self generated electricity in industry on the basis of CHP steadily decline. This decline was due to:

(a)   The economics of scale provided by large power stations.

(b)   Readily available cheap fuel (mainly oil) that more than compensated for the lower overall efficiency and relatively high distribution costs associated with large power stations. Cheap fuel could be used too for inexpensive steam raising in simple package boilers.

(c)   Labour costs rose much faster than electricity costs so simplicity overruled thermal efficiency.

Little surprise then that few CHP projects went ahead and those that did generated only enough electricity for internal use because suitable buyback agreements were difficult to arrange with electricity supply companies .

However, as a result of the two substantial oil price increases in the 1970's the economics of self-generated CHP improved due to:-

(a)   increasing fuel prices which put extra emphasis on system efficiency;

(b)   increasing capital costs for large power stations (delays, environmental concerns, etc.)

ELECTRICITY PRODUCTION BY COMBINED HEAT & POWER AS SHARE OF TOTAL ELECTRICITY GENERATION IN THE NETHERLANDS.

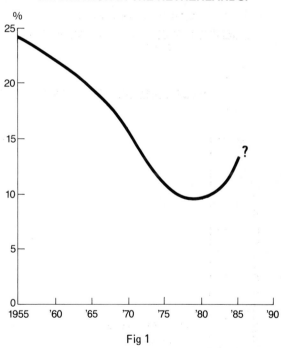

Fig 1

Further, it was realised that promotion of CHP increased energy efficiency and therefore improved the countries' overall energy balance and diversification.

A Government Commission to look into the potential of cogeneration reported in 1981 that:

(a)   Cogeneration offered major energy savings.

(b)   Potential market of 4.3 GWe (£1.5 billion).

(c) Attractive economics.

(d) Problems would be:
 – unfamiliar technology
 – lack of suitable financing arrangements.

(e) Natural gas fuelled turbines best present technology while coal fbc's offer a later option when technical/economic factors permit. Coal gasification/combined cycle units could be a future option.

(f) Electricity buyback by utilities required on a pre-arranged tariff basis.

(g) Natural gas availability must be guaranteed for at least ten years.

(h) Finance schemes and incentives would be required (off balance sheet, unsecured) to enable the technology to be introduced. Many industries were highly geared, that securing further debt was difficult and they had other priorities for their investment programmes.

So the Netherlands became the first country to include cogeneration with natural gas in their energy policy. The Netherlands were rich in gas reserves, it was available virtually everywhere at 40 bar and was relatively cheap.

INDUSTRIAL USE OF GASTURBINE POWER IN THE NETHERLANDS (SUBDIVIDED INTO POWER RANGES)

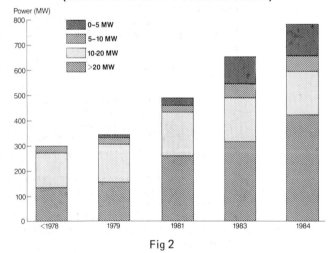

Fig 2

FUTURE GAS TURBINE POTENTIAL*† IN THE NETHERLANDS

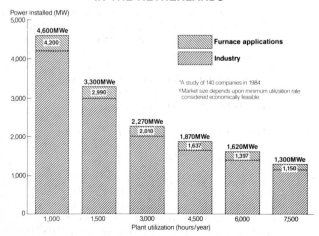

*A study of 140 companies in 1984
†Market size depends upon minimum utilization rate considered economically feasible

Fig 3

About 1200 MWe of gas fired cogeneration are now in place (total production capacity = 15,000 MWe) with prospects of 3000 MWe by the end of the century. The current cogeneration picture in the Netherlands has been reviewed by Van der Lugt[1]. Some of his data is reproduced in Figures 2 and 3.

Future possible markets were reviewed by Hellemans[2] of Vereniging Kraftwerktuigen. He analysed the market in terms of process steam pressure requirements and the degree of plant utilisation. His essential findings are summarised in Table 1 and Figure 4.

INDUSTRIAL USE OF GASTURBINE POWER IN THE NETHERLANDS (SUBDIVIDED INTO TYPE OF INDUSTRY)

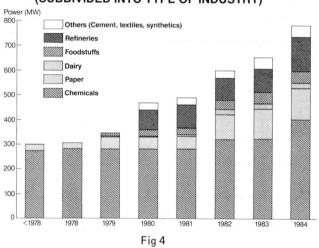

Fig 4

2 THE ENERGY MANAGEMENT COMPANY

Shell Industrial Energy Management (SIEM) was set up in response to the perceived need for a business that could offer service and help to industries with the relatively unfamiliar CHP technology and to provide the required finance. SIEM offers a complete service whereby they will take responsibility for some, or all, aspects of a customers energy utilisation. They specialise in providing all services related to the installation of CHP schemes from preliminary design through to operation, maintenance and provision of all the required capital costs. If one considers the value added chain for the production of heat and power shown in Figure 5, this is forward integration from fuel supply into service aspects of the business. Savings achieved by the introduction of CHP technology are shared between SIEM and the client in an agreed negotiated manner.

ENERGY MANAGEMENT VALUE ADDED CHAIN

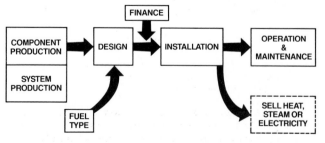

Fig 5

3 THIRD PARTY FINANCING CONCEPTS

Industries wishing to take advantage of the benefits of cogeneration are faced with three possible options for owning and financing a conversion project:

(a) Own and finance the project using personal equity or debt funds.
(b) Lease from another party but operate the plant itself.
(c) Engage the services of a third party* energy management company. Such a company can provide a complete service (design, finance, build, operate and maintain).

Many options and financial arrangements are possible between the industrialist and the third party energy management company. Therefore, every contract tends to be unique because it depends upon the services required, the equity share, and the amount of project risk and benefit sharing considered acceptable.

* THIRD PARTY

The industrial concern is first party; the utility who accepts and pays for excess power is second party; the energy management company that owns and (co)operates the cogeneration facility is third party.

Some possibilities are:-

(a) Joint venture.

The industrialist provides the site and the opportunity. The third party provides design, acquisition, construction and supervision. Joint venture is used to describe joint investment (50:50; 75:25) by both parties. The EM company would construct a turnkey power plant for the joint venture and provide supervision of operation and maintenance. The fuel could be supplied by either the joint venture or the industrialist. (See Figure 6).

JOINT VENTURE FINANCING

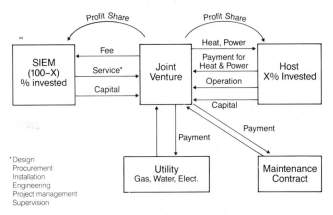

*Design
Procurement
Installation
Engineering
Project management
Supervision

Fig 6

(b) Shared Savings.

Under such a scheme the third party finances and owns the cogeneration facility that operates on the client's site.

The third party is responsible for all capital requirements, operation and maintenance. In some cases, the third party staff run the facility, in other cases they supervise the industrial staff. (See Figure 7).

THIRD PARTY OWNERSHIP WITH SHARED SAVINGS

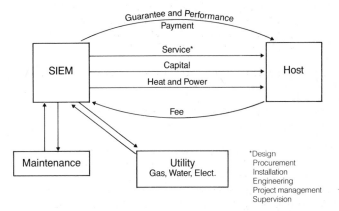

*Design
Procurement
Installation
Engineering
Project management
Supervision

Fig 7

Savings from the project are shared with the industrial client in accordance with a negotiated agreement.

Sometimes the payback to the client is split into two portions:

(i) a guaranteed return irrespective of the financial success of the venture, and
(ii) a performance bonus linked to the level of saving achieved by the project.

(c) Energy Sales.

The third party owner operator energy management company sells steam and electricity at an agreed price which need not bear any relationship to the cost of the investment or the savings achieved.

The price for the energy depends upon what the market will bear in relation to what the third party requires to recover his capital investment and make a profit. This is sometimes referred to as an energy services contract.

(d) Loan Scheme.

Under this scheme the third party design, build and operate (or supervise operation) of the plant on the industrial site. The industrialist owns the plant, paid for by the third party as a loan to the industrialist. Interest and capital repayment on the loan depends upon the performance of the new venture.

(e) Lease option (see Figure 8).

(f) Other Possibilities.

Sometimes contractual relationships are developed that are a combination of (a) – (e). These contracts can be extremely complex and differ considerably. However, certain generic elements are essential in most contracts. Some of these contract elements are:-

Contract must:

   (i)   offer a guaranteed cost saving compared with client's current situation;

  (ii)   define sanctions for non-performance by both parties;

 (iii)   define performance

  (iv)   include maintenance and supervision;

   (v)   define cost saving;

  (vi)   define minimum usage;

 (vii)   define limits to continuity of supply required (i.e. boundary conditions and who is responsible for reserve power);

In the USA where financing of cogeneration projects has become extremely innovative, other options have been used.

LEASE OPTION

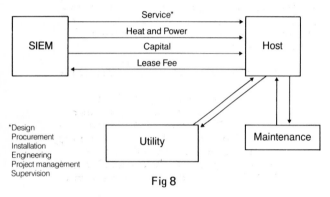

*Design
Procurement
Installation
Engineering
Project management
Supervision

Fig 8

4   SELECTION OF THE INSTALLATION

The initial choice of CHP configuration depends upon the heat to power ratio, efficiency of heat/power production and the desired prime mover. Table 2 gives some typical practical values for various CHP prime movers. Typical H/P ratio ranges for a number of energy-intensive industries are shown in Table 3. Gas turbines provide the most extensive coverage of the H/P ratios required. A selection of typical gas turbines and their main features are given in Table 4.

The process evaluation methodology is shown in Figure 9. The evaluation begins with an understanding of the likely inter-fuel prices, electricity costs and the $/Nfl exchange rate for the next ten years. Based upon a set of technical criteria for the required CHP system various equivalent technical options are evaluated for their capital cost and possible financing arrangements required. The best overall option is determined that depends upon technical choice, cost and financing arrangements. However, the most important feature is the profitability of the scheme after client guarantees and expected performance bonuses have been paid. Parameters such as simple payback, net present value, life cycle cost and internal rate of return are used to establish the attractiveness of each individual project. Each scheme is compared with the so-called "base case" that evaluates the cost of operating the existing plant

without any changes. Figure 9 shows the steps in this process in diagrammatical form. The best overall option is determined and an offer made to the client.

CHP – PROJECT EVALUATION

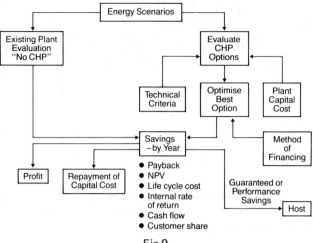

Fig 9

Certain issues that are important in determining the outcome of these calculations are given in Table 5.

5   A TYPICAL SCHEME

The first contract undertaken by SIEM was for a major brewery site in the central Netherlands. Built about six years ago the brewery is one of Europe's biggest and supplies at full capacity around 6.6m hl/year of beer (660,000 tons). The existing central boiler house had six gas fired horizontal shell boilers, each operating at 10 bars pressure and providing saturated steam at the rate of 25 tonnes/hr. While the steam demand of the plant varied considerably it averaged 35 tonnes/hr with occasional peaks to 90 tonnes/hr. The electricity demand averaged 8 MW but variations occurred between 2-12 MWe. Typical steam and electricity profiles observed are given in Figures 10, 11 and 12. The new plant had to be capable of matching these variable heat and power loads while operating in the most efficient possible mode.

TYPICAL STEAM & ELECTRICITY DEMAND – DAILY BASIS

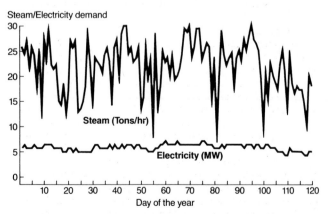

Fig 10

TYPICAL CHARACTERISTIC STEAM & ELECTRICITY DEMAND – TYPICAL INDUSTRY, TYPICAL DAY

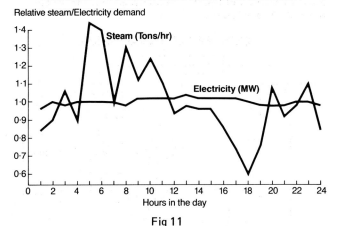

Fig 11

TYPICAL STEAM REQUIREMENT CURVE WITH ASSOCIATED ELECTRICITY DEMAND

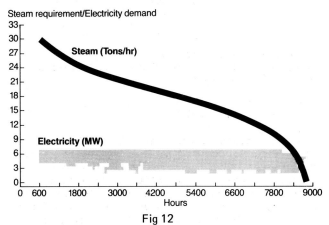

Fig 12

A number of power plant configurations with electrical power levels in the range of 7–12 MWe were evaluated for combined technical/economic performance. The selected CHP scheme used three Allison 501KB5 gas turbines packaged by CENTRAX. The CENTRAX package is a skid mounted gas turbine with generator, lubrication system, electrohydraulic start system, acoustical casing around the system, ventilation and air filters. CENTRAX refer to this package as the CX 350. Each delivers nominal power of 3.6 MW(e).

Several types of waste heat boiler were considered. Typical conditions required were:

Steam production
  (no supplementary firing)   12.7 ton/h
  (with firing)   29 ton/h
Steam pressure   13 bara
Steam temperature (saturated)   192°C
Feed water temperature   105°C
Gas turbine exhaust gas flow   15.6 kg/s
                 temperature   540°C
Max supplementary gas firing rate   1215 Nm³/h

Two of the gas turbine units feed their exhaust gases to respectively two new Breda water tube waste heat boilers having both economiser and evaporator sections. Each Breda boiler connects via pumped circulation to one of the existing shell boilers that serves as a steam drum. Gas fired burners on these boilers have been retained to supplement the gas turbine exhaust heat and to provide continuity in the event of turbine tripping. Steam supply

from each boiler with this arrangement is possible in the range 10–25 tonnes/hr.

The third turbine exhausts to a completely new boiler installation with supplementary gas burners firing a water cooled hearth. The existing waste gases from the gas turbine that enter the boiler combination contain about 15% oxygen which is sufficient to support combustion of the supplementary gas supply which increases the steam output flow from 10 to 35 tonnes/hr. Four of the original six boilers were retained as standby capability.

Two of the existing boilers were removed to provide space for the new layout to be integrated within the existing boilerhouse layout with otherwise minimum change. A schematic diagram is given in Figure 13.

A key feature of the system is the control equipment that measures, controls and records which of the several sources of steam should be used to satisfy the rapidly changing needs of the brewery at maximum efficiency while considering the status of the electricity import/export balance. The optimisation programme used permits a high degree of automated control as well as extreme flexibility.

The system is split into three parts:

(a) Optimising computer system with terminal, printer, VDU and savings control. The type FOX 300 from Foxboro controls takes care of energy management and communicates with several outstation "Microspec" modules via a FOXNET communication network.

(b) Two microprocessor based calculating/control outstations.

(c) Required in situ measurement instruments and control valves.

A Continental control/Centrax system takes care of the gas turbine/generator set programming and synchronisation etc.

The interface software regulates to ensure that the resulting operation leads to maximum possible cost saving while providing the requisite heat/power load. This is a key feature of the design.

At any moment, hourly and cumulative savings achieved by the plant are displayed and can be retrieved from the computerised management control system. Key operating parameters are measured, displayed on VDU monitors, stored and printed out on request. The basis of saving calculations is the cost of heat/power generated with the new CHP scheme in relation to the cost of energy from the existing operation (steam from inhouse boilers; electricity purchased from the local utility). With plant configurations similar to that described above all steam requirements and the greater part of electricity requirement for the energy intensive industries listed in Table 3 can be provided.

The brewery project was completed in June 1985 at a cost of £5.9 million. Availability of the system at the brewery during the first six months of operation was 97% with a total running time of 10,800 hours (total for three gas turbines). Problems that have been encountered were of a minor nature not connected with gas turbine operation. Emissions measured at the plant are well within the statutory requirements. Three other schemes are currently under construction (see Table 6) and all should be on line by the second half of 1986.

6   CONCLUSIONS

Shell Industrial Energy Management was established in 1983. It met a need pointed out by a Government study for off-balance sheet financing and technical know-how in the art of installing optimised combined heat and power installations on industrial sites in the Netherlands.

The business was assisted in its development by:-

(a) Ready availability of high pressure gas and the possibility of securing long term gas contracts.

(b) Government energy saving investment subsidies (32% to 13-12-83; 22.5% thereafter) available on this sort of project. These are expected to be phased out eventually.

(c) Relatively high electricity prices. These differ region to region based upon the fuel used (oil, gas, coal) to generate the electricity. Fair buyback rates have been agreed and long term contracts are possible.

(d) The Netherlands has a reasonable industrial tax rate (43%) and relatively low inflation (3-6%).

Since the Energy Act (1983) was introduced by the Government in the UK, industrialists installing CHP schemes can sell electricity back to the Electricity Boards. However, few schemes have been commissioned since 1983. Companies like EMSTAR[3], the Shell UK equivalent to SIEM, can provide the capital cost, expertise and are prepared to shoulder the risk associated with such projects. One must therefore look to gas supply issues and contracts, electricity buyback rates and contracts or lack of Government investment subsidies for the reason why CHP technology has not developed yet in the UK.

BREWERY COMBINED HEAT AND POWER PLANT

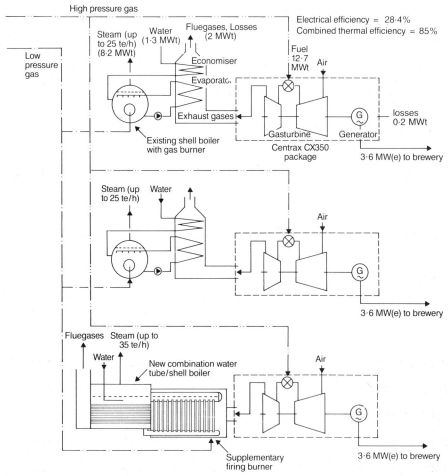

Fig 13

Table 1   Estimation of Gas Turbine Potential in The Netherlands

Boiler pressure range (bar)	Average Pressure	Steam Production A (t/yr)	Steam Production B (t/yr)	CONVERSION FACTOR KW/TONNES	G.T. POTENTIAL A (MW)	G.T. POTENTIAL B (MW)
1-10	8	60	81	420	25	34
11-20	14	919	1125	457	420	514
21-30	28	276	311	518	143	161
31-40	37	465	554	550	256	305
41-50	44	149	187	570	85	107
51-60	57	225	234	430*	97	101
61-70	68	254	264	448*	114	118
71-80	76	556	642	462*	257	297
1-80	±20	2904	3398	±480	1397	1637

*additional firing required   A - plant utilisation factor of 6000 hrs/yr

B - plant utilisation factor of 4500 hrs/yr

Table 2   A Comparison of CHP Options - Prime Mover Characteristics

	Efficiency		Heat/Power Ratio
	Electricity	Total	
Diesel Engine	40	50-90	0.2-1.3
Gas Engine	25-33	65-90	1.0-2.6
Gas turbine	20-35	65-85	1.6-3.3
+ suppl. firing	5-30	75-90	2.0-15
+ s.f. + steam	5-35	75-90	1.5-10
Boiler + steam turbine	5-17	94	4.5-18

Table 3   Typical Heat to Power Ratios for Certain Energy Intensive Industries

	MINIMUM	MAXIMUM	AVERAGE
BREWERIES	1.1	4.5	3.1
PHARMACEUTICALS	1.5	2.5	2.0
FERTILISER	0.8	3.0	2.0
FOOD	0.8	2.5	1.2
PAPER	1.5	2.5	1.9

Table 4

SOME GAS TURBINE OPTIONS FOR COMBINED HEAT AND POWER*

TURBINE/MAKE	POWER (KW)	GAS USE (m³/h)	EXHAUST FLOW (kg/s)	EXHAUST TEMP (°C)	ELECT EFFIC (%)	STEAM PRODN (kg/h)	RETRIEVABLE HEAT IN WHB (to 120°C) (Kwt)	NOx EMISSIONS (g/GJ)	TURBINE INLET TEMP (°C)	COMPRESSION RATIO –	GAS INLET PRESSURE (min bar)
ALLISON 501 KB5	3865	1463	15.8	532	28.4	10179	6965	157	1035	9.3	18.5
ALLISON 570-KA	4742	1813	18.9	557	28.3	13076	8835	76	803	12	20.0
ALLISON 571-KB	5627	1925	19.9	537	31.7	13010	8879	87	803	–	20
DRESSER CLARK DC 990	4264	1624	19.9	491	28.4	11290	7980	–	1035	12	15
FIAT AVIAZIONE LM 500	3940	1444	15.9	517	29.3	9789	6754	129	–	15	25
HISPANO SUIZA THM 1203	5440	2808	34.6	500	20.7	20179	14068	80	905	8.2	13
KONGSBERG KG5	3030	1622	21.0	503	20.4	12517	8639	187	–	6.3	11
RUSTON TB 5000	3525	1627	20.7	492	23.3	11757	8239	133	870	7.1	13.5
SOLAR CENTAUR	3130	1296	17.5	429	24.0	7838	5786	–	878	9	12

* About sixty gas turbine options exist in total in the Netherlands from about sixteen suppliers. The above list is typical but not exhaustive.

Table 5   CHOICE OF CHP/GT CONFIGURATION

ENERGY

Electricity, cost, buy back rate

Gas, availability, pressure cost, calorific value

Security of supply required

Electrical tie-in possibilities

Electrical tariff structure before/after CHP

- Reserve power cost
- Maximum demand cost structure

PLANT

Average heat, power consumption

Plant utilisation, hours per year

Range of heat/power demand ratio

Possible demand modification
- to produce extra savings
- H/P ratio modification

Turbine efficiency vs load

Boiler efficiency vs load

INVESTMENT ANALYSIS

Installed capital cost

Payback

Net present value

Life cycle cost

Internal rate of return

OPERATION

Experience of operators, costs

Space available

Training required

Environmental factors, noise, NOx

Maintenance costs

Table 6 Shell CHP Schemes in Progress

Type of Industry	Gas Turbine	Waste Heat Boiler	Control Systems	Size (MW)
Pharmaceuticals*	Allison 501 KB5(3x)	BREDA	FOXBORO	10.5
Fertilizers	Allison 571	STANDARD FASEL	ODS	5.5
Cocoa, Chocolate	Allison 501 KB5	STANDARD FASEL	HONEYWELL	3.5

* Combined Cycle

REFERENCES

1. Van der Lugt, WA

"The importance of gas fired turbines for
energy production and the environment in the
Netherlands. Energy Economy 84 Symposium,
Amsterdam, December 11th, 1984.

2. Hellemans, J. G.

Vereniging Kraftwerktuigen, Amersfoort.

A study of the potential of CHP in Netherlands
industry (1984) made on behalf of NEOM.
Published Sept. 30th 1985.

3. Prosser, R.M.B. "A joint venture CHP scheme
for a large brewery in the Netherlands."

Paper presented to the International Energy
Efficiency Conference, Brighton, September
1985.

ERRATA

Page 45

The details of the authors given immediately below the title of the paper should read as follows:

P C WARNER, CEng, FIMechE, FInstE, FBIM, Northern Engineering Industries plc, R A McFADDEN, BSc, Mainmet Holdings plc, R A J MOODIE, BArch, DipTP, Lothian Regional Council, G P WHITE, Associated Heat Services.

Pages 81 - 84

Following the recent fall in the oil price, the Preliminary Assesment Charts, Figs 9 - 11, have been modified to include an allowance for lower fuel prices. An additional chart for heavy fuel oil diesel plant (Fig. 11(a)) has also been included as these engines are now much more attractive.

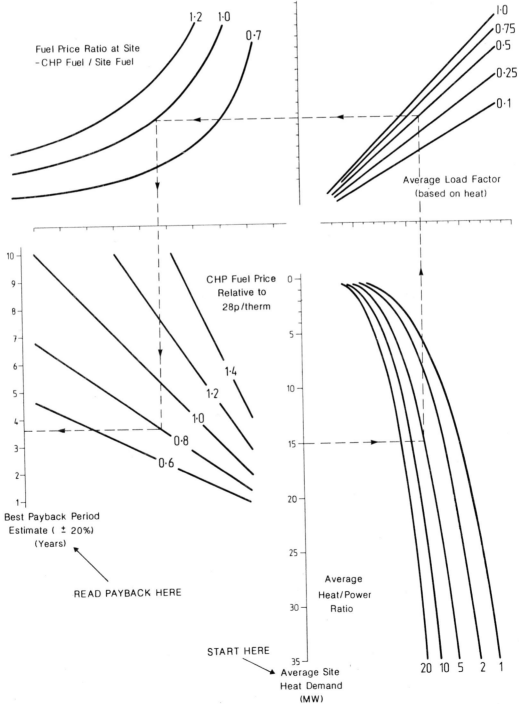

Fig 9   Preliminary CHP assessment chart — gas turbine plant
(based on 1985 capital costs)

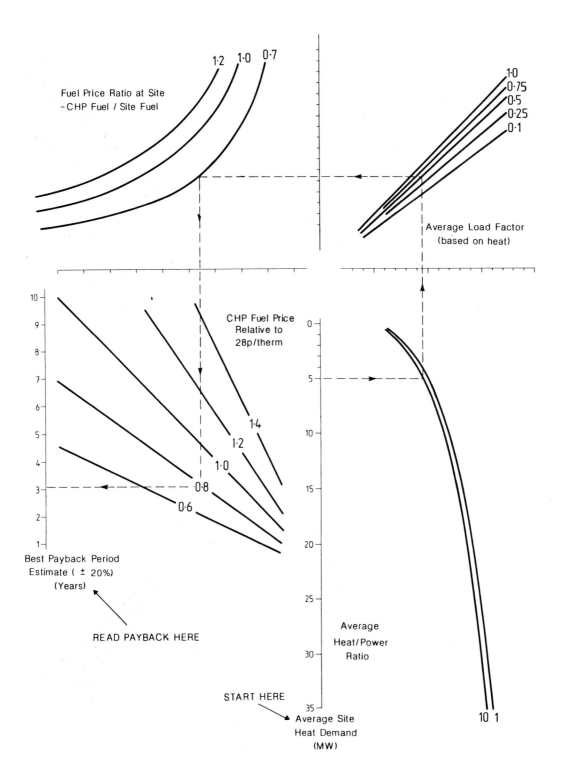

Fig 10 Preliminary CHP assessment chart — spark ignition engine plant
(based on 1985 capital costs)

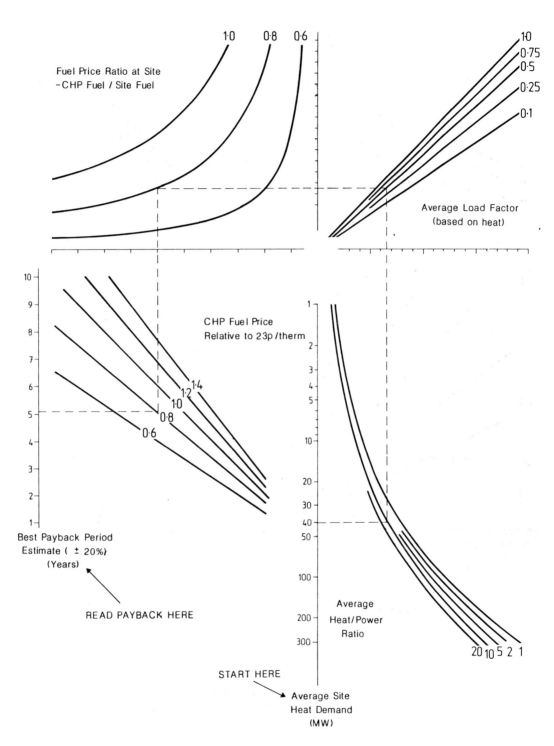

Fig 11 Preliminary CHP assessment chart — coal fired boiler/steam turbine plant
(based on 1985 capital costs)

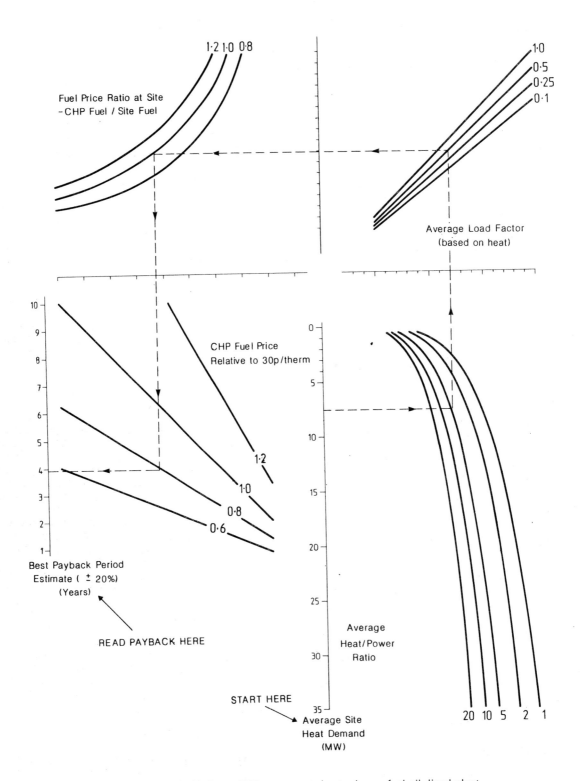

Fig 11a   Preliminary CHP assessment chart — heavy fuel oil diesel plant
(based on 1985 capital costs)

Bringing CHP/DH to two UK cities

P C WARNER, MA, CEng, FIMechE, FInstE, **R A McFADDEN**, BSc(Eng),
R A J MOODIE, BArch, DipTP and **G P WHITE**
Northern Engineering Industries plc

SYNOPSIS: Edinburgh and Belfast are two of the cities where the financial prospects for district heating from combined heat and power are being investigated by Consortia combining industrial membership (substantially the same for both) with strong local interests; the object is to learn whether city CHP schemes can appeal to the private investor. The paper deals with the historical build-up of interest in CHP in both places, leading to the formation of Consortia in response to a Government invitation, and the award of grant-in-aid announced in January 1985. It then explains how the two studies have been planned, and sets out their content: the key technical and commercial factors, and also the statutory and other more general considerations. The work is well under way, and the paper reports on progress, including field work to ascertain heat demand, the choice of fuels and sites for heat-only sources and for the combined plant, and the sequencing of implementation progressively across the city.

1. INTRODUCTION

The concept of Combined Heat and Power applied to District Heating (CHP/DH) has been demonstrated extensively in other countries and its thermodynamic principles are clear. A city uses both electricity and heat, traditionally derived separately: the electrical power from single purpose power stations and the heat in a variety of direct ways. The overall efficiency of electrical generation is limited thermodynamically to around 35%; the rest of the fuel energy is mostly in lukewarm water. Converting fuel into heat is not limited in that way and efficiencies can exceed 80%. So with separate systems, the overall efficiency would be 55-60%. CHP/DH is a single combined process that supplies to the city heat rejected from the power station at an efficiency of over 70%. It therefore saves fuel, but as in all energy conservation systems, this is counteracted by the cost of the engineering works to achieve it.

For various reasons, some controversial, CHP/DH is not used widely in the United Kingdom. Three studies are currently receiving Government support. This paper gives an interim report on two of them, Edinburgh and Belfast.

2. HISTORICAL BACKGROUND

2.1 From Marshall to Walker

Recent history of CHP/DH in the UK may be dated from the Marshall Committee reporting in 1979 (Ref. 1), whose recommendations are well known: a major one was to select a "lead city" to demonstrate CHP/DH. In response, Government invited local authorities in April 1980 to state their claims and 27 did. A short list of nine cities were investigated in detail by W. S. Atkins (Ref. 2).

There was further hesitation and debate, with the Select Committee on Energy taking a hand (Ref.3). Progress was fitful until April 1984, when the Secretary of State issued his now famous invitation (Ref. 4). Edinburgh and Belfast were among the respondents.

2.2 The Story in Edinburgh

The interest of Lothian Regional Council and Edinburgh District Council in CHP/DH goes back to November 1979. After the publication of Ref. 2 they formed a Joint Steering Committee to promote Edinburgh as a "lead city". It has twelve Councillors from both authorities and all political parties, with members from the South of Scotland Electricity Board (SSEB) and the National Coal Board; and an observer from East Lothian District Council (where Cockenzie is located). The SSEB also had been investigating CHP/DH, providing information on sites and plant to Atkins. They worked with Kennedy & Donkin on prospects in Edinburgh and Glasgow and reported jointly in May 1983 (Ref. 5).

Following the invitation (Ref. 4), the two Councils agreed to participate in an Edinburgh consortium: industrial partners were found, SSEB joined, and a submission was duly made (Table 1).

2.3 The Story in Belfast

Belfast was also one of the 9 short-listed cities, and Belfast City Council had been enthusiastic throughout about CHP/DH, but the limited powers of local government in Northern Ireland inhibited them from active promotion.

The Northern Ireland Economic Council (NIEC) had seen the potential of CHP/DH for Northern Ireland, and in September 1983 set up a Steering Group to study and promote it.

Working with the Northern Ireland Electricity Service (NIES), who had supported Atkins with specifications and costs of CHP plant for a Belfast scheme, they reported (Ref. 6) in January 1984 that the prospects for commercial viability were very favourable.

When the invitation came that April, NIEC catalysed formation of a Consortium (Table 2), and a submission followed.

2.4 Setting up the Projects

The essentials of the Government invitation (Ref. 4) were:

- the formation of local consortia of public and private sector organisations

- proposals for project studies of local whole city CHP/DH to establish its financeability in the private sector (loosely termed a "prospectus")

- up to three to be awarded half their costs, to a maximum of £250K

Among the ten consortia that submitted proposals, there were three whose industrial members were similar: those for Tyneside, Edinburgh, and Belfast. The last two were successful.

Both have consortium agreements in being and contracts with the Department of Energy were signed in August 1985. The members make their contributions through engineering and other work, costed without profit. Matching grant-in-aid of £250K brings the total sum to be expended to £500K for each city, and a proportion is available for external services. The two Consortia freely exchange information and results, and also with the Tyneside group (who are active though their submission was unsuccessful).

3. PRINCIPLES OF THE INVESTIGATIONS

3.1 Engineering and Commercial

An effective CHP/DH scheme has the following characteristcs:

(a) Adequate "high density heat load" (HDHL) typically within the 20MW/KM^2 contour (Ref. 1); with corresponding hot water distribution pipes and wet heating systems

(b) A progressive build up, with operation in the DH mode only, until the scale is commensurate with a suitable power plant (new or converted)

(c) conversion to the CHP/DH mode, to give the good fuel utilisation peculiar to it

(d) Since power and heat are products of a single process and allocation of costs is to some extent arbitrary, the electricity and heat organisations must co-ordinate their commercial policies despite a contractual boundary at the power station fence.

(e) The CHP plant treated as part of the generating plant inventory, having a place in the merit order, a firm power contribution, and an impact on the tariff.

(f) The ability to supply fluctuating heat and electricity demands, through the choice of flexible turbine generator types; supplementary heat-only boilers for stand-by and peaking - including those installed during the build-up of heat load; or thermal storage.

3.2 Financial Implications

Characteristics (b) and (c) in particular make funding a CHP/DH scheme somewhat unusual. It is a large project, implemented over many years, and Interest During Construction (IDC) is added to the estimates.

It is also a progressive one: excluding a cheap fuel like refuse, whose scope is limited, the individual DH phases would not be separately viable because of the capital cost of distribution hardware. But after the first year or two, when income from DH sales exceeds the cost of fuel and maintenance, there is a revenue contribution to IDC, i.e. partial servicing of the capital borrowed so far.

4. CONTENT OF THE PROPOSED STUDIES

The objective of each study is to prepare and assess the financial case. Each starts from two reports: Atkins (Ref 2), with chapters on Edinburgh and Belfast; and its own local report, either Ref. 5 or Ref. 6.

At the time of writing, we are nine months into a two year programme. This section describes the content for both as originally listed.

(a) **Marketing and Sales**
An early task is confirmation of the size, distribution and development over time of the high density heat demand in the city, as researched earlier (Ref. 2); it covers domestic, commercial, industrial and public sector consumers.

Later on attractive packages have to be worked out, tailored to different types of consumer and catering for equipment conversion, metering, maintenance, etc.; the effective price of heat from CHP/DH must be competitive with alternative ways of heating. Electricity from the system also has value, and the combined sales income, year by year, has to be computed and fed into the financial assessments.

(b) **Early Engineering Choices**
Stipulate the area for each successive phase and the heat load contained within it, and map out the distribution pipes, to suit the eventual arterial system; decide upon a heat source for DH operation (probably a heat-only boiler, destined for peaking and stand-by in the completed scheme); and its location.

In each city, choose from the alternative locations for the CHP station, and select also the type and size of generating units.

The most probable fuel is coal, but lignite is an option in Belfast; gas is not excluded for heat-only boilers in Edinburgh.

(c) **Environmental Constraints to be investigated**

Allowable limits for emissions, especially of particulates, sulphur, chlorine and oxides of nitrogen; the impact of topography, etc., on plume dispersal; routes for solid fuel supply and ash removal; means of ash disposal.

Effect of plant and pipe routes on noise and nuisance to inhabitants nearby and disturbance to traffic; locations must be compatible with development schemes for the roads and for services.

(d) **Quality Assurance**

The system must be safe and reliable, and enjoy the confidence of customers. The Q.A. programme will cover design and supply of plant, construction, and operation, and include recommendations for stand-by plant, spares and repair and maintenance services.

(e) **Implications of Integrated Operation and Control**

If the CHP plant is owned and operated by a Utility, with heat sold into a city distribution system that is separately owned, questions of tariff and security of supply would be covered by contract. However, on technical and operational matters, collaboration at arms length is not enough. For instance, allocation of elements of capital and operating cost common to electricity and heat involves judgement. In addition, the place in the merit order of a CHP station within an integrated electricity network varies according to instantaneous heat demand, because cost of production (essentially the fuel cost) depends on the proportion of heat and electricity in its output. So the operators make not only conventional decisions when to start up or shut down electricity production, but also how (in the light of that) to supply the heat load: by varying the output proportions of the turbine generators, by starting up some of the heat-only boilers on stand-by, or by drawing on storage. These plants are on both sides of the commercial boundary.

Running a CHP/DH system against varying and often unmatched heat and electricity demands involves marginal costs of different items of the plant, and requires an integrated control system.

(f) **Capital and Operating Costs**

For a comprehensive time-related costing, capital costs follow from the technical specifications for the plant and district heating network for each successive phase, and including the consumer installations (no matter how these are subsequently financed).

Operating costs would be calculated over the life of the system, for a limited number of alternative fuel price projections.

(g) **Organisational Structure**

A study of alternative organisation structures having mixed private and public participation, with accountability and safeguards. The functions are the design, construction, and commissioning of the scheme; possible extensions to it; and its operation and maintenance. A critical requirement is to give confidence to prospective investors.

(h) **Legal and Planning Requirements**

Review the legislative implications of CHP/DH, which for Scotland and Northern Ireland are not the same as for England and Wales. This covers inter alia the laying of street mains, land acquisition, and rating; an examination with the planning authorities of the approvals required by a CHP/DH system, and whether to pursue conventional planning procedures or a special Bill.

(i) **Economic and Financial Assessment**

Limited economic work accompanies the early engineering decisions, but in due course there must be an assessment of the profitability of the scheme as a whole. Funding requirements are computed year by year, and alternative sources are examined, and potential investors are consulted so as to arrive at the conclusions of the study.

5. **PROGRAMME AND PROGRESS**

In programming the above work content for each study, a first milestone is a "Reference Design" as a firm and self-consistent basis for detailed work on specifications, costs, and the implementation programme, and as a datum for major variants.

A stagger of some two months has been established between Edinburgh and Belfast to avoid taking similar judgements simultaneously in the two places. At the time of writing both projects are on time, a Reference Design for the former having been defined just before Christmas 1985. Progress on two substantive pieces of work deserves to be summarised here: the identification of the heat load and the choice of CHP plant. Also under way is the identification and sequence of individual DH phases. A solution exists in outline for the Edinburgh Reference Design, but not yet in a form suitable for presentation.

6. IDENTIFYING THE HEAT DEMAND

For both cities heat maps and load duration curves were available from Atkins (Ref. 2), who had employed local consultants for investigations on the spot. The same two firms were retained to confirm the data four years later (admittedly a relatively short time since the scheme must remain viable throughout life while customer habits may change, a point that reinforces the need for flexibility).

The heat demand from a property depends on its characteristics and the needs of the occupants. Equations derived from empirical data (Ref. 7) are used for domestic consumers to give annual heat consumption coefficients. In Edinburgh, to limit the new effort required, seven sample areas were selected representing three important types of domestic/residential property, using alternative questionnaires, kept deliberately simple to ensure a good response. In Belfast, a leaflet with introductory information about CHP/DH on a question and answer format was distributed in batches in a selected area in East Belfast, which is representative of housing types throughout the city, and followed in the three days following by a door-to-door survey. Local community leaders had been informed and the co-operation of residents was good: 75% response was obtained, which is excellent.

For institutional, commercial and industrial properties, survey data is more accurate. The technique is illustrated by a comprehensive survey on Tyneside involving major premises in the centre of Newcastle, from which selected results are given in Table 3. An average efficiency of 75% was arbitrarily used throughout to convert fuel consumption to useful heat (i.e. the prospective DH demand), and the cost per useful therm, including maintenance, was derived.

In Edinburgh, all the commercial/institutional properties surveyed are centrally heated to modern temperature standards. Forty completed forms were returned. Although there were large individual variations from the earlier data, the average was only fractionally higher. In Belfast the surveys are still going on at the time of writing.

The overall conclusion is that the heat loads determined for Ref. 2 are adequate for present purposes except in some areas in Belfast where there have been substantial changes in the number or types of buildings.

7. CHP PLANT

7.1 Engineering Principles

Steam turbines are the automatic choice for CHP/DH on the scale of a whole city. A great deal is known about design and operation of both back-pressure and pass-out sets, and the questions are whether to convert an existing power station, or build a special one; and if so, where that should be sited and what fuel it should burn; and either way, the type of plant and the unit size. Interaction with the electrical supply network makes the economics of CHP/DH quite complex; on the face of it, the CHP station should be part of its natural development, which favours solutions involving conversion of a station that exists or is already planned.

Fair progress with these questions has been made both at Edinburgh and Belfast.

7.2 Edinburgh CHP Station

The two sites available for the CHP station are Cockenzie and Seafield.

Cockenzie has 4 x 300MW(e) coal-fired units, which could be converted to pass-out operation by tapping steam from the IP/LP cross-over to give 200MW(h) from each set, with a loss of electrical output of 57MW(e). Pass-out conditions at full load are approximately 3.9bar and 270°C, which is 127°C of superheat. This pressure is high enough to ensure realistic DH supply temperatures over the potential range of heat and electrical outputs; an auxiliary turbine would be uneconomic. Previous studies (Ref. 5) proposed modifying two turbines, leaving one as standby. The outage period would be 3-4 months per machine, preferably in successive years taking advantage of annual overhauls.

Cockenzie has been selected as the CHP plant in the Reference Design, but its claims are not conclusive, as heat output with one machine converted is limited to 200MW(h); when the peak HDHL reaches 500MW this accounts for 85% of the heat consumption because of the uneven shape over time. It leaves a significant fraction of heat to be supplied by HOBs, and given the complex interplay of economics and load factors, together with the need for flexibility against changes in heat consumption habits, Seafield remains a possibility.

The site there is vacant ground partly recovered from the foreshore by landfill. There is single track rail access which would be developed for coal handling with a conveyor system. Environmental aspects are important. Flue gas desulphurisation (FGD) may be required. Initial estimates of building and chimney sizes suggest that a CHP station would be visually acceptable.

Pass-out sets can increase electrical generation at peak times, which is superficially attractive for Seafield, but given the characteristics of the Scottish network this flexibility may be of little value. Back-pressure sets give more heat per unit of electrical output and could achieve fairly high load factors. This is not yet resolved.

The pass-out design would be based on the set installed at Vaasa in Finland (Ref. 8). A back-pressure set would be sized for 275MW(h) at 95°C. It would be a two-cylinder reheat unit, with a single-flow HP cylinder and double-flow LP cyclinder having asymmetric flow paths. Steam conditions would be 160 bar abs, 538°C with reheat. Gross generation would be 170MW(e), giving 155MW(e) sent out.

7.3 Belfast CHP Station

The NIES network is not large, and the scale of a CHP plant to supply heat to the Belfast HDHL is commensurate with a new power station on their system. Their next major development, for commissioning in the mid 1990s, could be an extension at Kilroot (where civil works for units 3 and 4 are already in place) or a lignite fired station at Crumlin. The decision is linked to plans for the Province's lignite resources, and may not be taken until the present study is too far advanced to take account of it.

Given the timescale of a CHP/DH development, it is the next stage, for commissioning around 2000, that is directly relevant; possible sites are again Kilroot and Crumlin, and either could be built as a CHP station, probably with pass-out sets. On the basis that one of the two will be developed when the time comes, the Belfast CHP study is concerned with the incremental costs of CHP plants relative to conventional plants at each site. It may be that those increments are similar, even allowing for transmission costs.

8. CONTINENTAL EXPERIENCE

There are many CHP/DH schemes in Sweden, Finland, Denmark, Germany, France, and elsewhere. Some UK manufacturers have provided equipment, and a number of UK consultants are active, often in association with firms on the Continent. But we lag well behind in application and a consortium of UK organisations, however experienced in their individual fields, should not neglect Continental work.

Many Continental practitioners in CHP/DH have offered to help, and some useful visits have been paid notably to Denmark and Sweden. A number of relationships are being followed up.

A possible solution would be through a managing consultant. Appointing a different firm for each city might even tap a diversity of experience. However it is ruled out by the level of funding available and in any case does not lead to technology transfer.

One clear need was for a model to optimise the pipe distribution systems and select performance parameters and sizes; after a careful assessment, the Danish model Rørnet by B. Højlund Rasmussen (Ref. 9) was selected for Edinburgh and Belfast, and will be used also for the limited Tyneside work. It is in regular use to design and operate Danish installations.

The terminal at the offices of Orchard Partners in London has direct access to the computer network in Denmark, and this has been extended by a microcomputer and modem at International Research & Development in Newcastle (they are handling the systems work for both Consortia) so in effect there is direct access between IRD and the Danish computer system, and staff have been trained in the use of the programmes.

Another mechanism for technology transfer from Continental practice is the Design Audit; the argument is that design work within British companies, whatever its intellectual and technical merit, may contain flaws that would be discovered only during building or operation. The Continental engineering developments will have paid the usual price for ideas that did not work out in practice: there is no substitute for having lived through it. Through a Design Audit, an experienced Continental operator would say whether any of the paper proposals had in fact been tried and found to contain a flaw.

9. CONCLUSIONS

CHP/DH is a process with two products, each with a solid demand largely uncorrelated with the other and subject to fluctuations with times and seasons. The key to successful exploitation lies in supplying the major part of the heat load with the CHP plant, i.e. in circumstances where its electrical output also provides cost benefit, while keeping to a minimum the use of high fuel cost heat sources. The right balance has to be achieved both over time, during the relatively long period in the DH mode when the heat load is being built up, and for the completed scheme.

Consequently early work at Edinburgh and Belfast has concentrated on the information critical to that: an understanding of the make-up of the heat load and its variations; and assessments of the alternative CHP plant options and sequences for implementation.

Satisfactory progress is reported in this paper, with a Reference Design now available for Edinburgh and the Belfast programme set some two months behind. Both projects are on course for the objective of reporting on financeability in the private sector, in early 1987.

REFERENCES

1. Energy Paper No. 35
   Combined Heat and Power and Electrical
   Power Generation in the United Kingdom –
   Report to Secretary of State for Energy
   by the Combined Heat and Power Group.
   Department of Energy, 1979

2. Energy Paper No. 53
   Combined Heat and Power District Heating
   Feasibility Programme: Stage 1
   Summary Report and Recommendations
   by W S Atkins & Partners.
   Department of Energy, 1984
      (Report first submitted 1982)

3. Combined Heat and Power –
   Third Report from the Energy Committee,
   Session 1982-83
   House of Commons Paper 314, April 1983

4. Statement by the Secretary of State for
   Energy, Mr. P. Walker, 5th April 1984

5. Combined Heat and Power Associated with
   District Heating – A Study of Alternative
   Schemes for Edinburgh and Glasgow
   by South of Scotland Electricity Board
   and Kennedy & Donkin Associates.
   SSEB, May 1983

6. Combined Heat and Power: The Belfast Case
   Report of the CHP Steering Group.
   Northern Ireland Economic Council,
   January 1984

7. Data from the Institute of Heating and
   Ventillating Engineers' Guide, Table B4.11

8. Appendix to submission by
   Northern Engineering Industries plc
   to the Select Committee on Energy,
   March 1981

9. Optimisation of DH-Systems
   Claus Højlund Rasmussen,
      B. Højlund Rasmussen
   Paper to seminars on District Heating and
   Energy Systems Management,
   Columbus, Ohio & San Francisco October 1985

Table 1

MEMBERSHIP OF EDINBURGH CONSORTIUM

Associated Heat Services Plc
Fairclough Scotland Ltd.
Mainmet Holdings Plc
Northern Engineering Industries plc
Press Construction Ltd.

Lothian Regional Council
Edinburgh District Council

South of Scotland Electricity Board
Scottish Development Agency

Noble Grossart are retained as financial
advisers without consortium membership.

Table 2

MEMBERSHIP OF BELFAST CONSORTIUM

Associated Heat Services Plc
Fairclough Scotland Ltd.
Harland & Wolff Plc
Mainmet Holdings Plc
Northern Engineering Industries plc
Press Construction Ltd.

Northern Ireland Electricity Service

Ulster Investment Bank (financial advisers)

Belfast City Council could not be members,
but have made a significant cash grant.

Table 3

TYPICAL RESULTS FROM TYNESIDE HEAT SURVEY

Reference No.	Gas Therms pa	Oil Litres pa (Type)	Coal Tonne pa (Type)	Useful Therms at 75% effy	Gas p/therm	Oil p/litre	Coal £/tonne	Maintenance Costs £ pa	Total Costs £ pa	Cost per Useful therm p
1	175,000			131,250	34			400	59,900	45.64
2	831,000			623,250	34			3000	285,500	45.81
3			8000 (Ash'ton)	1,769,858			70	52,000	612,000	34.58
4			760 (Ash'ton)	168,136			70	6,000	59,200	35.21
5	200,000			150,000	34			3,000	71,000	47.33
6	315,900			236,925	34			3,000	111,400	47.02
7	28,400			21,300	37			500	11,000	51.64
8	55,877			41,908	32			400	18,300	43.67
9	150,000			112,500	33			2000	51,500	45.78
10	40,000			30,000	32			1000	13,800	46,00
11	22,700			17,025	37			500	8,900	52.28
12	69,000	15,000		55,800	34	20		500	27,000	48.39
13		5,375,862 (3500 sec)		1,578,487			16	40,000	900,100	57.02
14	40,000			30,000	33			800	14,000	46.67

The economic evaluation and engineering of a co-generation plant for a leather works

P S WOODS, MA, CEng, MIMechE, MInstE and **A J MORROW**, CEng, FIMechE
Orchard and Partners, London
N A PEARCE, BEM
W Pearce and Company Ltd, Northampton

SYNOPSIS

The results of a feasibility study of a Co-generation plant based on spark-ignition gas-engines are described. The influence of future fuel prices on the economic case is discussed and modifications to the electricity tariffs proposed. The method of approach to the design and selection of the plant is also considered.

1. BACKGROUND TO POWER GENERATION AT BILLING PARK SINCE 1938

In 1936 the Leather Producers, W. Pearce & Co. (Northampton) Ltd. decided that a new tannery should be built on a greenfield site in the grounds of Billing Park. At the design stage thought was given to the energy requirements of the new works, and the most economical means of providing it.

At the time, all Power Stations were producing power utilising not more than 25 - 28% of the total energy input the balance of 72 - 75% being lost up the chimney stack and from the cooling tower.

The production of leather requires considerable quantities of hot water for the various processes, and it seemed entirely valid to consider whether the hot water requirement could be met by generation of power and the recovery of the waste heat.

At the time, little consideration had been given to heat recovery, and it needed some courage to embark on such a scheme, as well as a great deal of persuasion if contractors were take the matter seriously.

Fortunately the English Electric Company were, if a little reluctant at first, prepared to undertake the design of a Power Station based on the use of two of their 6K engines, the scheme being capable of being extended to double the original output with four engines.

The highly successful design of a 6 cylinder 600 RPM 300 Horsepower engine was directly coupled to a 256KVA 0.8 P.F. 415V 3 phase English Electric Alternator with a tandem exciter.

The heat recovery equipment comprised two sets each capable of dealing with one engine. The jacket water leaving the engine was fed into a Clarkson thimble tube waste heat boiler, the water leaving the waste heat boiler going to the hot side of a heat exchanger and thence to the engine driven water pump to repeat its circuit. The process water entered the cold side of the heat exchanger and after recovering the jacket water heat is pumped to the hot water process tanks.

The designed overall efficiency was 80% and on test working at 83% output, 78.65% thermal efficiency was obtained.

Over the period June 1938 to September 1985, some 47 years, the plant has continued to give excellent service though, due to the escalation in the price of oil by a factor of ten, and the deterioration in the heat recovery installation, the cost of power and hot water had become unacceptably high.

Knowing that the plant was nearing the end of its useful life in 1984, consideration was given to replacing it. With the advent of the Energy Act 1983 the prospects for private generation were enhanced, and the concept of Combined Heat and Power Schemes (CHP) became widely accepted as providing a realistic answer to escalating energy costs. An indepth CHP Feasibility Study was commissioned which showed clearly that it was possible to have a payback period of about 4 and a half years and it was decided to replace the existing plant with a gas fuelled plant which would run as a baseload unit in parallel with the EMEB mains and at times feed into the Board's Network.

It was also decided that a Department of Energy Demonstration Grant should be sought and this paper sets out the stages leading to the present scheme and the awarding of a demonstration grant.

2. ASSESSMENT OF HEAT AND POWER DEMANDS

The first stage of the feasibility study was to obtain data on the demands for heat and power at the site. In addition to the demand for process water, steam was produced from two shell boilers fired on HFO, mainly to operate drying cabinets. Typical hot water quantities were obtained by assessing the number of batch processes for each type of leather, and using previous measurements of the process water requirements for each. Power demands were assessed by taking hourly readings on ammeters and also by installing an automatic recorder over 1 week. Typical demands were estimated as follows:-

Power   : Peak 450 kW, average 350 kW

Hot Water   : 23,000 gallons per day, equivalent to 20 GJ per day or 617 kW on average for 9 hours.

Steam   : 43,500 lbs steam per day, equivalent to 58 GJ per day or 1,790 kW on average for 9 hours.

The demand profiles over the day were also estimated which showed that hot water demand was highest in the morning period and that power consumption was relatively steady except for the lunchtime period. Steam demands were also highest at the start of the day in order to bring the driers up to temperature.

The CHP plant can only be sized to the average hot water demand if there is sufficient storage capacity to smooth the demand. There are two 5,000 gallon storage tanks on site and it was possible to show that these would be adequate even if a 'worst case' draw-off rate applied. An operating period for the CHP plant of 9 hours, similar to the power demand period, was assumed so that the heat demand on the CHP plant was estimated to be 617 kW on average. Two plant options were examined, one producing slightly more than 617 kW, the other one, as a result of the unit size available, producing 520 kW heat.

3. THE COSTS AND BENEFITS OF CHP

After an initial comparison of possible CHP plants including diesel and steam turbines it was decided that a spark-ignition gas-engine would be the most appropriate for the heat to power ratios of the site demands. The diesel plant was rejected due to the high fuel cost at the time of the study and the steam turbine on the grounds of capital cost,

as additional boiler capacity would be required.

In order to evaluate the cost savings with CHP it is necessary to assume the cost of heat production without CHP. Normally this is the current cost, but as the existing diesel plant was coming to the end of its life the alternative heating method would be from a shell and tube heat exchanger supplied with steam from the boilers. Although the boilers are currently fired on HFO, a conversion to gas was assumed with an overall efficiency of 75%.

The basis for the plant sizing was to meet the total hot water demand from a 9 hour operating period. The information supplied by two manufacturers (A and B) is given in Table 1 which also shows the hourly operating cost benefit assuming full heat utilisation and no export of power (at 1984/85 prices). In practise, the size of plant selected results in a small export of power in the lunch period and at the beginning and end of each day. The effect on the annual operating cost benefit was found to be small. Assuming a 240 day working year, and a 9-hour operating period, the total benefit available from CHP is :

A : £16,350 p.a.
B : £14,020 p.a.

Further operating savings can be made however:

i) Maximum Demand Charge

    For a site operating on a single shift and with relatively few running hours for the plant, the saving of the maximum demand charges becomes important. It was decided to arrange for one of the existing diesel generators to be retained in the scheme so that, even if one of the gas-engine units failed, no additional power import would be required. The extra savings generated would then be:

    A : £3,607 p.a.
    B : £4,142 p.a.

ii) Power Export

    Under the Energy Act 1983, it is possible to sell electricity to the local electricity board, in this case the East Midlands Electricity Board (EMEB). Even if no useful heat can be taken from the engines, a cost benefit could be obtained over 3 winter months when the tariff is particularly high. Additional income obtained by generating power between about 1630 and 2000 hours for December, January and February was :

    A : £1,080 p.a.
    B : £1,430 p.a.

The CHP plant would increase the gas demand significantly, to above 250,000 therms p.a., and EMGAS were prepared to make the supply to the CHP plant and the steam boilers on an interruptible basis This resulted in an additional saving for the site of:

A : £8,100 p.a.
B : £8,500 p.a.

The major operating cost is for planned maintenance work and, on the basis of an external maintenance contract, these costs were estimated at :

A : £2,500 p.a.
B : £2,800 p.a.

The overall economic case for CHP is given in Table 2.

4. OTHER ENERGY INVESTMENT OPTIONS

Although the economic case for CHP appeared attractive, it was necessary to consider whether alternative investments would be more worthwhile. These investments were also assessed against the modified demands arising from energy conservation proposals. The next best options to CHP were :

a) Existing boilers fired on gas, with economisers and heat recovery from the water effluent both supplying the process water

b) Replace existing boilers with new coal-fired plant, process water being supplied by the steam heat exchanger.

The economic comparisons of the three options which include the costs and savings from the energy efficiency measures are given in Table 3.

If grants could be obtained of up to 25% of capital for the CHP or the coal option then payback periods would be reduced.

The economic assessment showed that if capital was available up to £140,000 and payback periods below three years were acceptable, then the CHP and coal packages would be preferred to the heat recovery option. The difference between coal and gas-engine CHP was small and could be reversed, as the grant for the coal plant was likely to be smaller than for an ETSU demonstration grant for CHP. In addition, unusually, coal-fired boilers would represent a more major change in the method of energy supply at the site, compared to reciprocating engine CHP plant. For these reasons it was decided to apply for an ETSU demonstration grant, and, if this was obtained, to pursue the CHP option. The CHP plant option effectively enables a more convenient fuel (gas) to compete with a lower cost fuel (coal).

5. FUTURE FUEL PRICES

Each of the supply options was examined in the light of the fuel price projections presented by the CEGB and supported by the Department of Energy at the Sizewell Inquiry. These showed that gas prices were likely to rise faster than coal or electricity prices, and this would favour coal-fired boilers rather than CHP. However, the rate at which rises in gas price might occur is uncertain, and there a stronger link between gas and oil prices for the industrial sector might be expected. With the current depressed oil price situation, the prospects for relatively stable gas prices in the short to medium term would be enhanced.

Even if it is decided that the gas plant is preferable to coal, once the plant is installed the investment may be at risk from changes in fuel and electricity prices. A CHP plant has two advantages here however. Firstly, because two income streams are generated changes in one have less effect, and secondly, the alternative source of heat supply (gas-fired boilers) will be subject to the same fuel price changes. Each plant was examined to compare the operating saving that would occur under fuel and electricity price projections, and the results are shown in Figure 1. Even though the overall costs would rise, the savings against the alternative route for supplying heat remain approximately constant for plant A, but decrease for plant B. This difference is explained by the higher overall efficiency of Plant A. The calculations for a 15% increase in gas price and no change in electricity price are given in Table 4. This shows that operating costs would approximately double, but that the savings generated would decrease by 10.5% for Plant B but only 4.1% for Plant A. Thus plant A might be preferred even though the payback period at current fuel prices is longer.

Plant B was examined in more detail to evaluate the savings for different overall efficiencies; as indicated in Figure 2, if the overall efficiency is improved then the risk of future fuel price rises reducing savings would not be so great. The advantage that gas-fired CHP plant has is in the linking of CHP fuel price to the competitor heat price; the main risk is then dependent on a relative fall in electricity prices. Conversely, coal-fired CHP plant shows a linkage between its fuel price and electricity costs (being mainly coal related at the margin) and is most at risk from a fall in the alternative heat price.

6. OPERATING DETAILS

The basis for the operating system is to utilise stratified storage tanks. Cold water is drawn from the base of the tanks and from the cold feed, circulated through a heat exchanger and returned to the top of the tank. In the early part of the day when draw-offs are high, the level of cold water will rise. As the engines continue to run the cold level will fall until the tanks are full of heated water again. At this point, the engines will shut down automatically as their cooling load reduces to zero. In the peak winter months however, air-cooled heat exchangers will remove the engine heat once the process demand has been met, until a timeclock shuts down the engines at 2000 hours. Should one of the gas-engines fail, the existing diesel plant will be brought into operation, operating in parallel with CHP plant but isolated from the EMEB.

Additional standby would be provided from the steam heat-exchanger on the heat side and the EMEB for power, the latter being used in preference to the diesel plant in the summer months.

The detailed design stage will evaluate the hot water demand profile and the plant sizing in order to establish :

a) whether the existing heat stores are adequately sized to permit a 9 hour operation period,

b) whether the operating hours could be extended to permit a smaller size plant to be installed, thereby increasing the running hours and the economic performance,

c) whether it would be economic to install additional storage capacity so that smaller plant could be used and operated for a longer period.

Monitoring is currently in progress to assess the demand profiles in more detail. A typical daily profile is shown in Figure 3. The results of a recent monitoring exercise on small-scale CHP in a hotel application (1) showed that a smaller plant would have shown more attractive paybacks; it is therefore recommended that detailed measurements of heat demands should be undertaken before selecting a CHP plant size, and that undersizing is to be preferred to oversizing.

7. SELECTION OF EQUIPMENT

As discussed above, the performance and capital cost of the CHP plant will form the basis of a comparison between suppliers. Other important aspects are discussed below:

Reliability is not always given sufficient weight in plant selection mainly because its effects are difficult to quantify in terms of comparative operating costs. For a CHP plant, poor reliability decreases the possible savings by increasing replacement energy costs and incurring capacity charges.

In this area particularly there is no substitute for experience, and the selection process will include pre-qualification of potential suppliers on the basis of numbers and operating experience of successful units.

Maintenance and reliability are closely linked, and good maintenance (like good operation) will tend towards maximum reliability. The economics of setting up an on-site maintenance facility with trained staff for one or two units is unlikely to prove attractive and the best approach is considered to be a maintenance contract, if possible linked to extended guarantees.

The economic performance of all energy conversion plant depends on its achieving predicted thermal perform-ance and availability for at least the life span assumed in the calculation of financial returns. Engine design parameters such as shaft speed and BMEP, together with general design features, give some indication of robustness, but once again experience is the keyword. As for reliability, selection processes will include a review of numbers and machine years for each candidate engine. Here it is recognised that the application of spark-ignition technology has resulted in the appearance on the market of a number of packages using engines previously operated on liquid fuels and that these packages have not been in service long enough to demonstrate longevity. A rational approach is to take full account of the experience of the generic line of these engines in assessing the gas-fired derivative and, although some difficulty is anticipated, this will be done.

8. SYSTEMS DEFINITION

Currently design work is continuing, in preparation for the issue of enquiries.

In particular the various aspects of integration into the existing electrical system are being examined in order to ensure that the installation complies with the Electricity Council's Engineering Recommendation, G59(2). Close liaison with the East Midlands Electricity Board is anticipated to finalise this work. The generators will operate in parallel with the Board's system and at times will export power. G59 sets down fault conditions under which a unit must be disconnected and regulation governing the drawing of starting power from the grid.

For most of their operating time, the generators will run at full output to charge the storage tanks with hot water. A thermal trip will shut them down at preset cooling water temperature, except at times when the tariff makes straight generation worthwhile. Under these conditions the standby cooling system will allow continual generation within proscribed time bands. Control philosophy will be drawn up to comply with these broad requirements. Other issues not yet resolved include such aspects as the need for uninterrupted supply in the case of grid failure during CHP plant operation.

9. DISCUSSION

An application was made for a 25% capital grant through the Energy Efficiency Demonstration Projects Scheme (EEDPS) administered by the Energy Technology Support Unit (ETSU) at Harwell. This involved writing an account of the proposed installation and making an economic case containing sufficient detail so that the results could be verified by independent checking. A number of sensitivities were calculated which resulted in payback periods ranging from 2.7 years if HFO was used for the alternative heat cost and 6.2 years if interruptible gas was supplied both before and after the CHP plant was installed.

The provision of an ETSU grant enabled a decision to be taken with more confidence, given the improved payback periods and the additional checks made on the proposal and its economics. The more widespread introduction of CHP in industry could be assisted further by the EMEB as follows:

A change in the tariff for imported power to a unit rate system, once CHP is installed. Such unit rates are already published and apply where transfer of power to other sites is undertaken. This would reduce the penalty for outages which occurs under the maximum demand charge system. For example, if 100 kW of generated power is lost for one half hour in any month, the 50 kWh imported would currently cost (EMEB, 1985)

  519p/kWh in December and January
  364p/kWh in November and February
  4.02p/kWh in other months.

If a number of small CHP plants is installed, then the probability of simultaneous failure will be low. Using the unit rates from the purchase tariff (3) for MOD (3) (available to consumers with maximum demands outside peak periods) the penalty for the 50 kWh import would cost at most :

29.29p/kWh in December, January
        (4 p.m. to 7 p.m. only)
 5.29p/kWh in November and February,
 3.90p/kWh in other months.

It is suggested that these prices reflect the costs to the area board more accurately than applying a maximum demand charge. The result of such a charge would be less uncertainty in the savings predicted and enhanced economics, particularly for industrial plants on single-shift working.

There appears to be provision within the tariff for metering costs to be

met by the EMEB and recovered by additional monthly charges. In view of the different financial criteria between a public sector body and a private company it would appear to be to the advantage of the company if the EMEB could meet the initial capital cost of any modifications required on other parts of their equipment or local network and recover the cost, with appropriate interest by means of monthly charges.

It would also be appropriate under the Energy Act, 1983 for the EMEB to be involved directly in the purchase of the CHP plant itself, selling on both electricity and heat.

10. CONCLUSIONS

a) The feasibility of installing a gas-engine CHP plant must take account of operating savings, maintenance

b) A gas-fired CHP plant with a high overall efficiency will, in general, be less at risk from gas price rises.

c) Penalties on the maximum demand charge basis are particularly onerous for a CHP installation and modifications to the tariff arrangements might assist CHP development.

11. REFERENCES

(1) FEC Consultants Totem Total Energy System in a Hotel Interim Report ED/70.161 Energy Technology Support Unit, January 1986.

(2) System Development Consultancy Group. Recommendations for the connection of private generating plant to the Electricity Board's distribution systems Engineering Recommendation G59, The Electricity Council, Chief Engineers' Conference, June 1985.

(3) East Midlands Electricity Board. Tariffs for private generators/ suppliers 1st April 1985.

Table 1 - Performance and Operating Benefits from CHP Units

	PLANT OPTIONS	
	A	B
Total installed power (kW)	270	310
Number of units	3	2
Fuel Rate (kW)	1,015	1,087
Heat output (kW)	630	520
Cost of fuel/hour (£)	11.64	12.46
Saving in heat cost/hour (£)	9.63	7.95
Saving in power cost/hour (£)	9.58	11.0
Net operating benefit/hour (£)	7.57	6.49
Reduction in heating cost (%)	79	82

Table 2 - The Economic Case for CHP

	Plant A	Plant B
Capital (£)	130,000	110,000
Total operating benefit (£p.a.)	29,140	28,392
Maintenance costs (£p.a.)	2,500	2,800
Net saving (£p.a.)	26,640	25,592
Payback period (years)	4.9	4.3
Real IRR (%)	17	19

Table 3 - Economic Comparisons of Energy Options

Option	Saving p.a. £	Capital Cost £	Payback Period Years
1. Gas/Heat Recovery	32,570	52,700	1.6
2. Coal	50,670	124,200	2.4
3. CHP	50,800	138,500	2.6

Table 4 - Effect of 15% increase in Gas Price on CHP

	Plant			
	A		B	
Costs/Revenues for each hour of operation	Current Price	+ 15% Price	Current price	+ 15% Price
Fuel for CHP	11.64	13.39	12.46	14.33
Electricity Credit	9.58	9.58	11.00	11.00
Net Operating Cost	2.06	3.81	1.46	3.33
Heat Cost from Boilers	9.63	11.07	7.95	9.14
Net Saving	7.57	7.26	6.49	5.81
% change in net saving	0	-4.1	0	-10.5

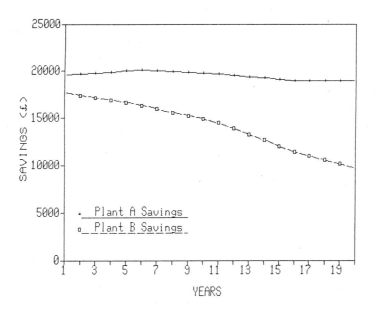

Fig 1   Savings generated by CHP over 20 years

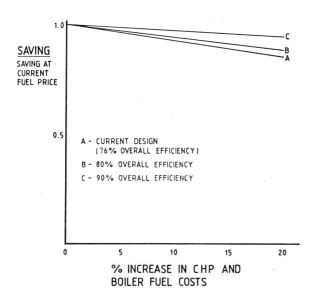

Fig 2   Plant 'B' savings for fuel price increases
(Note: no change in electricity credit assumed)

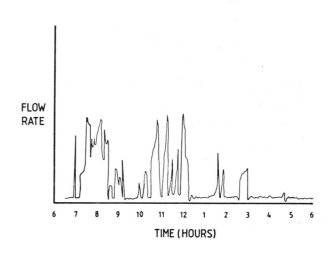

Fig 3   Pattern of process water demand

Industrial combined heat and power - investment savings and decision making

J D GURNEY, BSc, FIMechE, MRAeS, FCIBSE, FInstE, FInstR, MASHRAE, **R G F HYDE**, MA,
S J PICKERING, BSc, PhD, AMIMechE and **M SHUTE**, BSc, MSc, MPhil, Dipl. d'Ing, AMIMechE
Energy Group, Ove Arup and Partners, London

SYNOPSIS The economics of industrial CHP schemes are complex and require careful evaluation. A method of assessing CHP schemes by computer, which has been found to give good results, is described which enables the most cost effective CHP plant configuration to be determined as an aid to decision making and investment.

1   INTRODUCTION

Industrial combined heat and power (CHP) is not currently the main focus of attention for CHP protagonists in the United Kingdom. It tends to take a back seat behind city wide CHP combined with district heating and micro CHP. Nevertheless industrial CHP has been around in various forms for over a century and with the current interest in energy efficiency, especially by the Government in 1986 Energy Efficiency Year, the financial and energy savings offered by industrial CHP require serious consideration.

In the past industrial CHP schemes have been of two kinds: (i) where a relatively small quantity of electricity (in relation to the site demand) was generated from a steam turbine acting to reduce the pressure in a process steam line; (ii) where the 'total' energy requirements of a site were provided by a central heat and power station and with no connection to the national electricity grid (1). Few schemes, except for the largest at some chemical works, exported electricity from the site as the payments made by the electricity boards were not considered to be sufficiently attractive.

Since the Energy Act (1983) the electricity boards have been obliged to publish tariffs which offer realistic payments for electricity supplied to them by private generators. This is beneficial to industrial CHP as cost effective CHP plants may now be installed which match the heat demand of a site and at the same time give a reasonable return for any exported electricity.

The British Gas Corporation have also recently changed their policy and the price of gas is no longer dependent upon the type of the plant consuming it.

These two factors have both served to make investment in industrial CHP more attractive and have resulted in a change of emphasis from 'total energy' plants (1), (2) to those which exchange electricity with the local electricity board.

Characteristics for an Industrial Site

For a CHP plant to be economically viable it must operate at or near full load for a large proportion of the time. Many industrial processes operate for 8000 hours per year and have a steady heat demand that, unlike a demand for space heating, does not vary significantly with the season.

However there is frequently a demand for high grade heat such as steam commonly at temperatures up to 250°C and for furnaces at temperatures up to and sometimes well above 1000°C. Care must be taken to ensure that the most appropriate type of CHP plant is selected because different types of plant produce heat at different temperatures.

Industrial sites vary in size considerably. Sites which are very large consumers of energy, such as those in the chemicals and iron and steel industries already have well established CHP. It is at the medium sized sites with annual energy bills in the range £1-10m where many opportunities may be found. These sites typically have average heat demands in the range of 5-25 MW and are most suited to CHP prime movers of up to about 10 MW.

There are some industries where CHP plant has been removed in recent years. This has usually been steam turbine plant which has become obsolete on account of a falling heat demand. In these industries it may now be worth considering an alternative type of CHP plant with a lower heat to power ratio, such as a gas turbine.

There are three commonly available prime movers suitable for industrial CHP installations. These are: gas turbines; internal combustion engines and steam turbines. They may be characterized by three fundamental parameters:

- Heat to Power ratio
- Quality of heat output
- Fuel type

A summary of the characteristics of each type of prime mover is shown in Table 1.

2.1   Gas Turbines

Shaft efficiencies up to 35% (based on lower calorific value) can be obtained. All of the recoverable heat is in the exhaust gases at a temperature of about 500°C.

The exhaust gases contain a high proportion of oxygen so that after-firing can be employed to raise the temperature still further. The exhaust gases may be passed into a heat recovery boiler where steam or hot water may be generated. Alternatively the exhaust may be used directly in a process where it can substitute a hot gas stream.

Gas turbines are commonly available to run on natural gas or light distillate oil. At present natural gas is considerably cheaper than distillate and would be preferred. A disadvantage of a gaseous fuel is that it must be injected into the gas turbine at a high pressure, up to 20 bar absolute in some cases. Unless the gas is supplied at a high pressure a gas compressor must be used and this can absorb a significant proportion of the output power of the turbine, up to 10% in some cases.

2.2   Internal Combustion Engines

These may be compression ignition (diesel) or spark ignition and can be used with a variety of liquid and gaseous fuels. Shaft efficiencies of 30-45% (based on lower calorific value) can be obtained. The higher figures are available from large diesel engines.

The exhaust gases can be passed through a waste heat boiler to produce steam or hot water. Low temperature hot water at about 80°C can be recovered from the jacket cooling system. The exhaust gas temperatures are in the range of 300-500°C for diesel engines and 400-600°C for spark ignition engines. Diesel engine exhaust contains a significant proportion of oxygen and can be after-fired, whereas spark ignition engines cannot be after-fired.

For diesel engines heavy fuel oil is the cheapest liquid fuel and engines greater than 500 kW shaft output are commonly available for this fuel. When a gaseous fuel is used a light oil pilot fuel, amounting to 5-10% of the total fuel consumption, is also required to provide the ignition.

Spark ignition engines can operate on petrol or gaseous fuels. Natural gas is the cheapest widely available fuel for industrial applications.

Packaged CHP plants based upon vehicle-derived spark ignition engines are available with outputs from 15 to 100 kW shaft power. These are often more suitable for commercial installations. Larger industrial spark ignition engines are available in sizes from 100 kW to 2 MW shaft power.

2.3   Steam Turbines

In an industrial CHP application steam is exhausted from a steam turbine at a pressure suitable for a process application. The turbine is then referred to as a back pressure turbine, or passout turbine if steam is removed at more than one pressure.

The shaft efficiency of a back pressure steam turbine depends upon the pressure ratio and is typically in the range of 5-15% resulting in relatively high heat to power ratios.

The steam can be supplied from existing or new boilers. Existing boilers will often be of shell and tube construction and may not be capable of providing steam at a high enough pressure for a cost effective scheme.

Boilers can be operated on almost any fuel of which coal is the cheapest.

2.4   Combined Cycle Plant

The most common type of combined cycle CHP plant comprises combinations of gas and steam turbine plant.

The exhaust gases from the gas turbine are used to raise steam in a waste heat boiler which is then passed through a back pressure steam turbine. More electricity can be generated than in a single cycle gas turbine plant. Consequently higher shaft efficiencies and lower heat to power ratios can be achieved.

The cheapest most widely available fuel for these combined cycle plants is natural gas.

2.5 Choice of Plant

The choice can be narrowed down to the six most cost effective combinations which utilize the most widely available, well proven technology and the cheapest fuels (1986 prices):

Plant Type	Fuel Range Available
1. Gas Turbines	Natural Gas
2. Diesel Engines	Heavy Fuel Oil
3. Diesel Engines (Dual fuel)	Natural Gas/Light Oil
4. Spark Ignition Engines	Natural Gas
5. Boilers and Steam Turbines	Coal
6. Gas Turbine/ Steam Turbine Combined Cycle	Natural Gas

The industrialist is faced with identifying the most cost effective of these six CHP plants (and the use of any waste derived fuels) and selecting the optimum size of plant for the site under consideration.

3   ECONOMICS OF CHP

Appendix

The cost benefits of CHP result from the simultaneous on-site generation of heat and electricity and, in some cases, a change in fuel. A comparison of the costs that should be assessed is shown in Figures 1a and 1b. The net cost benefit is the difference in total cost shown in Fig. 1a and Fig. 1b.

There are a variety of methods for assessing the cost effectiveness of an investment. By far the most common method is simple payback. Other more sophisticated methods involving discounted cash flow can be used but simple payback is the most widely understood and will be referred to throughout this paper.

The economics of CHP depend crucially on the manner in which the plant is operated. It is important that the plant is operated in the most economical way at all times taking into account the variations that occur from time to time on a site. Cost effective operation will depend on the interaction of four principal factors:

(a)   The energy demands of the industrial site.
(b)   Fossil fuel and electricity prices.
(c)   The performance of the CHP plant.
(d)   The manner in which the plant is operated.

3.1   Site Energy Demands

The CHP plant is used to meet:

- the site electricity demand;
- the site heat demand

and any surplus could be exported profitably. It is important to know the temperature required to meet the heat demand as this can affect the amount of heat recovered from the CHP plant. Internal combustion engines can produce high temperature heat from the exhaust gases but only low temperature heat (usually <85°C) from the cooling water system. When internal combustion engines are investigated, it is useful to consider both low and high temperature heat demands.

It is crucially important that these energy demands are assessed as accurately as possible. This is discussed more fully in section 4.

3.2   Energy Prices

The price of the CHP plant fuel relative to the price of the existing fuel at the site is of prime importance. The savings will be much reduced if the CHP plant requires a more expensive fuel.

The electricity tariff varies with the time of day and season of the year. Electricity purchased at night is about half of the price of day time electricity and during the winter maximum demand charges are imposed. These variations and the payments made for exported electricity can determine the most economical mode of operation and should be carefully considered.

3.3   Performance of CHP Plant

The performance characteristics of greatest importance to the economics are:

- Heat to power ratio
- Overall CHP plant efficiency
- Changes in efficiency at part load
- Temperature of the heat from the CHP plant
- Turndown limit
- Maintenance requirements and costs.

The most cost effective CHP plant will match the site demands to provide the greatest savings for a given capital cost.

3.4 Identifying the Most Cost Effective CHP Plant

In view of the complex interrelationships between the site requirements, energy prices and the CHP plant type it is difficult to produce any guidelines that would immediately enable the most cost effective CHP plant to be identified.

The best method for assessing the cost savings resulting from a proposed CHP plant is to calculate hour by hour throughout a year the most economic way of operating the plant and to sum the savings over the whole year. This is the only method that can properly take into account all of the hour by hour changes in site energy demand and electricity tariff and establish the optimum mode of operating the CHP plant in each case.

Hence a computer program is the most appropriate method of determining the annual savings for a CHP plant. The speed of a computer means that many different CHP plants can be assessed relatively quickly and the most cost effective plant identified.

4 SITE DATA

The correct site input data is crucial for making a realistic assessment of a CHP plant. Carefully assessed daily profiles are needed in order to establish the most economical mode of operating the plant.

Experience has shown that it is easy to establish the total annual energy consumptions for fossil fuel and electricity as these quantities are measured accurately by the supplying authorities. It is much more difficult to establish typical hourly heat and electricity demands without detailed monitoring of the site over a year, which is expensive and time consuming.

A convenient method for estimating the hourly demand profiles that has been found to give acceptable results is to estimate the daily profiles in terms of a percentage of the maximum demand. The actual demands (in kW) can then be calculated from the total annual consumptions. This method has been found to be much more appropriate than trying to estimate the hourly demands directly in kW (without long term monitoring) as invariably the demands are over estimated and the annual consumptions are too large.

It has been found that, in the absence of long term monitoring, the minimum data requirement to make an initial CHP assessment should be as shown in Fig. 2. Typical demand profiles for three day types (summer, winter and non-working) are sufficient for an analysis in the absence of more detailed monitoring.

5 COMPUTER ASSESSMENT OF INDUSTRIAL CHP

The computer program has been written to perform an hour by hour CHP analysis and to calculate the payback period for a CHP plant at an industrial site operating in the most economic mode. The program can be run many times with different types and sizes of CHP plant, calculating payback periods in each case, from which the best plant may be identified.

5.1 Optimum Mode of Operation

A CHP plant may be operated in three modes:

(1) Electricity matching
(2) Heat matching
(3) Switched off

It is assumed that there are always heat-only-boilers that can be used as an alternative or as a supplement to the CHP plant whenever it is economic to do so. Further, that electricity can at any time be imported from or exported to the local electricity board and that the electricity board will provide a 100% standby to the CHP plant.

Electricity Matching - In this mode, the plant matches the electrical demand of the site. The heat output is used to meet the heat demand of the site and heat-only-boilers are used to supplement the CHP plant if necessary or heat may be dumped if the plant produces too much heat. If the electricity demand is too small to be met by the CHP plant even when operating at full turndown then it is switched off and electricity is imported. Electricity is also imported if the CHP plant is not big enough to meet the demand.

Heat Matching - In this mode the CHP plant matches the heat demand of the site. The CHP plant may be supplemented with heat-only-boilers or if the heat demand is too small to be met by the CHP plant it is turned off and heat-only-boilers are used instead. Electricity is exported or imported as necessary.

Switch Off - In some circumstances it is most economic to switch the CHP plant off and this option is always considered.

Choosing the mode of operation - The program calculates the running cost (made up of the costs shown in Fig. 1b) for each mode of operation for each hour of each day of the year.

It is not considered practical for the mode of operation to change every hour and so the day is split into three periods corresponding to the three electricity tariff periods of a winter peak day:

(a) midnight to 07.00
(b) 07.00 to 20.00
(c) 20.00 to midnight

The hourly running costs for each mode are summed over each period of the day and the mode with the lowest running cost selected for each period. Electrical maximum demand charges are included as appropriate. The mode of operation can therefore change not more than three times during the day.

The total annual savings include allowances for plant breakdown and maintenance and any maximum demand penalty that may be incurred as a result of plant breakdown. The annual savings represent the difference between the total running costs at the site with and without the CHP plant.

Using the heat and power demand profiles for typical summer, winter and non-working days, the program calculates another two interseasonal day types. These demands are calculated by assuming that the differences between winter and summer vary in proportion with published variations in degree days.

The program considers the utilization of the waste heat in the exhaust from the CHP plant and includes a procedure for calculating the quantity of heat that would be recovered from a waste heat boiler at both full and part loads taking into account the temperature at which the heat is required and the variations in heat transfer within the boiler as the exhaust gas conditions change.

5.2 Input Data - Site

This is shown in Fig. 2.

5.3 Input Data - CHP Plant

The CHP plant data consists of performance, capital cost and energy cost data as shown in Figure 3. Data has been collected on CHP plants of each of the six types described in section 2.4. It is organised into a database from which details of any commonly available CHP plant within the size range of 0.1 - 10 MWe electrical output can be drawn. In the case of internal combustion engines and steam turbines the range of sizes available from manufacturers means that almost any size of machine is available. Restricting the smallest size increment to 100 kW it is possible to draw data on over 1500 CHP plants. If multiple unit installations are considered the number is proportionately larger.

In the case of steam turbines the program contains data for representative single stage and multi-stage steam turbine and boiler combinations with boiler pressures up to 900 psig/900°F and covering a range of backpressures from 30 to 250 psig.

The variation of plant performance at part load is accounted for by assuming a linear variation between full load (maximum continuous rating) and the maximum turn down of the machine. This linear approximation results in errors of less than 5%.

The capital costs represent typical costs for a complete installation and include, where appropriate, the cost of new buildings, the provision of fuel supplies and storage facilities, connecting into the heat and electrical distribution systems of the existing site, contingencies and design fees. A general diagram showing capital costs for CHP plant is shown in Figure 4.

The energy costs include the price of fossil fuel for the CHP plant and existing heat-only-boilers. The electricity costs included a conventional maximum demand tariff and a private generation tariff.

Maintenance costs and allowances for maintenance and breakdown periods are included.

5.4 Use of the Computer Program

Two versions of the computer program are available as shown in Figure 5.

Version I
This analyses each of the six different types of CHP plant at a site. For each type of plant several sizes are analysed by incrementing through the size range. The following alternatives are considered each time.

(a) Installation of up to 4 units of plant (all units of equal size)
(b) Use of unfired or after-fired waste heat boilers
(c) Use of boiler economisers

The program analyses over 600 configurations of CHP plant and the installations which show a payback period of less than 10 years are shown on a printout, see Figure 6. The printout presents payback period, savings, capital cost etc. and enables the most cost effective plant to be identified which may be defined by:

(a) lowest payback period
(b) greatest running cost savings
(c) greatest Net Present Value

or some other criterion.

Version II
This performs the same analysis as Version I but for only one specified CHP plant. A detailed printout is given (Figures 7 and 8) which shows a breakdown of the fuel usage, running costs and savings as well as a table indicating the mode of operation of the plant on each of the day types and at each period of the day.

6 CASE STUDIES

Three case studies are presented for typical sites in the paper making, frozen food and brewing industries to illustrate the method and results achievable from the CHP computer program. Typical demand profiles and consumptions for sites with annual energy bills of £1-10 million have been used. The data does not relate to any particular sites.

The energy consumption data for each site is presented in Table 2 and the key results for each site shown in Tables 3 - 5.

6.1 Site Data

Papermill - The papermill has an annual average heat demand of 8.7 MW and an electricity demand of 2.7 MW. The heat to power ratio of 3.2 is a typical of many industrial sites. The site working hours are 24 hours/day and with 28 non-working days/year. The demand profiles are fairly constant throughout the day and as the demands are mainly for process use there are only small seasonal changes. The heat demand is met entirely by steam at 120 psig and 85% of the condensate is returned hot to the boiler. The only demand for low temperature heat that can be supplied by the cooling water from an internal combustion engine is for preheating the boiler make-up water and amounts to 140 kW on average.

The site uses gas in its boilers.

Frozen Food Factory - The site in the frozen food industry has an annual average heat demand of 7.0 MW and an electricity demand of 7.6 MW. The heat to power ratio of 0.9 is unusually low on account of the large electricity demand for refrigeration in this industry. The site working hours are 24 hours/day and with 120 non-working days/year. The demand profiles are fairly constant throughout the day and there is a significant electrical demand for refrigeration on non-working days. The heat demand is met by steam at 100 psig and there is a small demand for low temperature heat amounting to 700 kW on average.

The site uses oil in its boilers.

Brewery - The brewery is much larger with an annual average heat demand of 33.0 MW and an electricity demand of 8.9 MW. The main heat intensive processes operate for only 12 hours/day and there are 62 non-working days/year. The heat demand is met with steam at 100 psig and there is a demand for low temperature heat of 2.3 MW on average.

The site uses oil in its boilers.

Fuel Prices - The following prices were used in the analysis:

Interruptible Natural Gas	29p/Therm
Heavy Fuel Oil	12p/litre
Coal	£63/Tonne

The London Electricity Board Tariff for 1985/86 was used.

6.2 Results

The key results of the computer assessments for each site are shown in Tables 3-5. For the purposes of simplifying the discussion dual-fuel engines and combined cycle systems have not been included. Similarly only single unit CHP installations are considered.

The case of small back pressure steam turbines retrofitted to existing boilers has not been considered. There may be some sites where it is possible to place a steam turbine in the main steam line. This would be in place of a pressure reducing valve or where it is acceptable to raise the boiler pressure or reduce the steam distribution pressure. A detailed site investigation is necessary to establish the feasibility of doing this.

The payback periods shown assume that a completely new CHP plant is installed and that the existing boilers are retained. There may be cases where a boiler may need replacing in any case and so part of the cost of the CHP plant could be offset.

Paper Mill - (Table 3)

The CHP plant with the lowest payback period is a 4.8 MWe gas turbine with an unfired heat recovery boiler. The rating of this turbine is considerably larger than the average electricity demand and over a third of electricity generated is exported. The cost savings/kWe for a smaller turbine would be larger, as less electricity would be exported, however the larger turbine has a much lower capital cost/kWe. The average heat demand of the site is only 8.7 MW and so the benefits of after-firing the turbine exhaust gases cannot be fully realised.

Spark ignition engines show longer payback periods than gas turbines as there is little utilization of the engine cooling water. The smaller engine shows greater cost savings/kWe as a greater proportion of its engine cooling water can be utilized. Nevertheless the larger engine has a lower capital cost/kWe and gives a lower payback period.

The heavy fuel oil diesel engines show relatively poor cost savings/kWe as little engine cooling water can be utilized and heavy fuel oil is slightly more expensive then gas.

Even allowing for the cost savings resulting from the change to a cheaper fuel the heat demand is too small for the most economical sizes of coal fired boiler and steam turbine CHP plant.

Frozen Food Factory (Table 4)

This site uses heavy fuel oil for raising steam and although oil is more expensive than natural gas the cost savings at this site are lower than at the papermill. This is because there are 168 non-working days which is considerably more than the papermill, consequently the load factor for a CHP plant is reduced. The CHP plant with the lowest payback period is a 500 kWe spark ignition engine.

The most cost effective spark ignition engines are small and larger savings can be achieved with gas turbines although the payback period is longer. The low heat demand on this site means that the larger gas turbine cannot be fully utilized and so the payback periods are longer.

The heavy fuel oil diesels show relatively long payback periods. Again this is because little engine cooling water can be utilized.

Coal fired boiler and steam turbine plant is not economical as the heat demand is too low.

Brewery (Table 5)

The brewery site has the highest average heat demand, of 33 MW, of which a significant proportion, 2.3 MW, can be met at low temperature. Heavy fuel oil is used in the existing boilers.

The heat demand is high enough for economical sizes of coal-fired boiler and steam turbine CHP plant to be installed and the largest annual cost savings can be achieved by a 4 MWe multi-stage turbine. The savings result partly from the on site generation of electricity and partly from the change to a cheaper fuel.

The large heat demand makes after-fired gas turbine CHP plants particularly attractive and the change to a cheaper fuel enhances the savings.

Heavy fuel oil diesel engines offer greater savings/kWe than on either of the other two sites mainly as a result of the full utilization of the engine cooling water. Heavy fuel oil is more expensive than natural gas and so the savings are not as large as those for gas fired plant.

The smaller spark ignition engines, are the most economical because they meet the base load throughout the year, including non-working days.

The relationship between capital cost and plant size on payback period is shown to have an important effect in these case studies. Figure 4 shows that, almost universally, capital cost decreases with increasing plant size. The result is that lower payback periods can often be achieved from plants larger than those which would achieve the greatest running cost savings.

6.3 Detailed Output from Computer Program

Tables 3-5 present results from Version I of the computer program. Version II provides a detailed output showing the mode of operation of the plant and a breakdown of the costs and energy consumptions.

Two such printouts are shown for heavy fuel diesel engines at the brewery site, Figs. 7 and 8. They show the most cost effective mode of operation for the CHP plant.

Version I of the program takes a broad sweep across the ranges of CHP plant and increments through the sizes in fairly coarse steps. In Version II any size of plant may be chosen, which allows a particular engine to be investigated. For instance, Figures 7 and 8 refer to a 3.3 MWe diesel engine with unfired and after-fired exhaust gases. They demonstrate most clearly the feature of the program which chooses the most cost effective mode of operation. The after-fired plant remains in operation at night whereas the other should be switched off.

Electricity is cheaper at night and the benefits of CHP are reduced. After-firing the engine exhaust gases increases the overall efficiency of the plant, by over 10% in this case, and it becomes economic to run the plant at night.

7 PRELIMINARY ASSESSMENT CHARTS

The use of a computer program to assess the viability of industrial CHP requires the collection of fairly detailed data on an industrial site. It is considered useful for a preliminary assessment method to be available that would identify whether or not is is worth proceeding to this deeper investigation.

Part of a recent study on industrial CHP for the Energy Efficiency Office has involved the use of the computer program to investigate the economics of CHP on typical sites across a wide range of industries. A spin-off from this work has been to obtain correlations between the payback period, for the most cost effective CHP plant, and some simple parameters which characterize a site. The correlations are expressed in the form of charts, Figures 9-11, for gas turbine, spark ignition engine and steam turbine CHP plant. Four parameters are used to characterize a site:

(i)   Annual average heat demand,
(ii) Annual average heat to power ratio,
(iii) Annual average load factor of the heat demand,
(iv) Price of the CHP plant fuel relative to the price of the fuel used for the existing boilers at the site.

A fuller description of the use of the assessment charts is provided in Appendix 2.

It has been found possible using these charts to estimate the most cost effective payback periods to within ±20% of those calculated by the computer program. They were derived from data from the results of computer assessments of over 100 typical medium sized industrial sites (with energy bills greater than £0.5 million) and so the energy demand characteristics of many industrial sites are contained inherently within the charts. They should only be used for similarly sized sites and not for commercial establishments where the heat demand is dominated by space heating requirements. The computer program may be used for commercial sites however.

As the charts are so general they should only be used as a guide in making a preliminary assessment of CHP at an industrial site. The resulting payback period should indicate whether or not further investigation is worthwhile.

8   CONCLUSIONS

The main points can be summarized as follows:

(a) Recent changes in electricity tariffs, industrial gas prices and the general interest in energy efficiency encourage a fresh look at industrial CHP.

(b) There is a wide range of CHP plant types and configurations that may be considered for an industrial site.

(c) The economics of CHP depend up on a number of factors and a detailed hour by hour matching of the CHP plant to the site demands is the best way of determining the most cost effective mode of operating a CHP plant.

d) The use of a computer program is an effective low cost way of assessing many different CHP plant configurations to identify the most cost effective installation.

e) Accurate results depend upon the use of correct input data and the minimum requirements for site data are suggested.

f) A graphical method for obtaining a preliminary assessment of the payback period for CHP at industrial sites has been derived. This can be used to find out whether it is worth proceeding to a more detailed assessment.

9.   ACKNOWLEDGEMENT

The authors would like to thank the Energy Efficiency Office of the Department of Energy for their permission to publish material within this paper and also the many manufacturers who have supplied us with data on CHP plant.

10   NOMENCLATURE

kWe)   Electrical power demand and
)   installed net electrical
MWe)   capacity of a CHP plant.

11.   REFERENCES

1.   GURNEY, J.D. PEARSON, J. The total Energy Installation at John Player and Sons. *Total Energy Conference*, Brighton, Institute of Fuel, November 1971.

2.   GURNEY, J.D. Industrial Combined Heat and Power - A Case History. *National Energy Managers Conference*, National Exhibition Centre, Birmingham October 1978.

APPENDIX 1

Use of the Preliminary Assessment Charts

The charts are described in section 7 and shown in Figures 9 - 11.

Four parameters are used to characterize a site:

- Annual average heat demand (H_t)
- Annual average heat to power ratio (H_p)
- Annual average load factor (L_f) (based on heat demand)
- Price of the CHP plant fuel relative to the price of the fuel used for the existing boilers (F_p)

These parameters are defined more fully as:

$$H_t = \frac{AB \times 1000}{8760 \times 3600 \times 100} \quad \text{(MW)}$$

$$H_p = \frac{AB}{C \times 100} \quad \text{(dimensionless)}$$

$$L_f = \frac{H_t}{D} \quad \text{(dimensionless)}$$

$$F_p = E/F \quad \text{(dimensionless)}$$

Where:

A = Annual boiler fuel consumption (GJ)

B = Seasonal boiler efficiency (%)

C = Annual electricity consumption (GJ)

D = Typical maximum steady heat demand (MW)

This is the steady heat demand during a typical day at the time of year when the heat demand is highest. This is likely to be the winter period and a typical day would not be the coldest but an average day in December, January or February. An example of a typical maximum steady heat demand is shown in Fig. 12. It should be noted that short peaks such as the warm up period are not included. Experience from a number of sites has shown that the typical maximum steady heat demand will always be lower than the installed boiler capacity of a plant and often in the region of 50% - 80% of the peak heat demand during the warm-up period.

E = Price of fuel for CHP plant (£/GJ)

F = Price of fuel for existing boilers (£/GJ)

Table 1   Characteristics of Prime Movers for CHP

Primer Mover	Heat/Power Ratio	Quality of Heat Output	Most Common Fuel
Gas Turbine	1.5 to 5.0:1	Hot gases 500°C	Natural gas Light Oil
Gas Turbine (with after-fired exhaust gases)	Up to 15:1	Hot gases 500 to >1000°C	Natural gas Light Oil
Internal Combustion Engine (heat recovery from exhaust gases)	0.5 to 1.0:1	Hot gases 300 to 600°C	Natural gas Any oil
Internal Combustion Engine (heat recovery from exhaust gases and cooling water)	0.8 to 2.0:1	Hot gases 300 to 600°C Hot water 80°C	Natural gas Any oil
Internal Combustion Engine (with after-fired exhaust gases and heat recovery from exhaust and cooling water)	Up to 5:1	Hot gases 300 to >1000°C Hot water 80°C	Natural gas Any oil
Back pressure steam turbine	>5:1	Steam up to 250 psig (18 bar abs)	Coal, Gas, Oil or wastes

Table 2   Site Data for Case Studies

Site	Paper Mill	Frozen Food Factory	Brewery
Annual electricity consumption	24200 MWh	66600 MWh	77600 MWh
Annual fossil fuel consumption for boilers	3500 kilotherms	3300 kilotherms	12800 kilotherms
Average electricity demand	2.7 MWe	7.6 MWe	8.9 MWe
Average heat demand (total)	8.7 MW	7.0 MW	33.0 MW
Average heat to power ratio	3.2	0.92	3.7
Quality of heat from boilers	Saturated Steam 120 psig	Saturated Steam 100 psig	Saturated Steam 100 psig
Average heat demand at low temp < 85°C	0.14 MW	0.64 MW	2.3 MW
Proportion of steam condensate return	85%	60%	80%
Efficiency of existing boilers	74%	77%	77%
Number of non-working days per year	28	120	62
Existing fuel at the site	Natural Gas	Heavy Fuel Oil	Heavy Fuel Oil
Annual energy cost without CHP	£1.9 million	£3.2 million	£7.0 million

Table 3   Results of CHP Assessment at Paper Mill

Plant Details	Plant Capital Cost [£/kWe]*	Annual Site Running Cost Savings [£/kWe]*	Annual Site Running Cost Savings [%]	Payback Period [years]
Gas Turbine 3.1 MWe	493	105	17.5	4.7
Gas Turbine 3.1 MWe with after-firing	534	118	19.6	4.5
Gas Turbine 4.8 MWe	454	101	25.9	4.5
Gas Turbine 4.8 MWe with after-firing	488	105	27.0	4.6
Spark Ignition Engine 390 kWe	505	84	1.7	6.1
Spark Ignition Engine 540 kWe	453	79	2.3	5.8
HFO Diesel Engine 3.1 MWe	417	61	9.8	6.9
HFO Diesel Engine 3.1 MWe with after-firing	499	84	13.6	5.9

*   Cost expressed per kWe of installed capacity of CHP plant.

Table 4   Results of CHP Assessment at Frozen Food Factory

Plant Details	Plant Capital Cost [£/kWe]*	Annual Site Running Cost Savings [£/kWe]*	Annual Site Running Cost Savings [%]	Payback Period [years]
Gas Turbine 3.1 MWe	493	89	8.7	5.5
Gas Turbine 3.1 MWe with after-firing	534	104	10.2	5.1
Gas Turbine 4.8 MWe	454	100	15.0	4.5
Gas Turbine 4.8 MWe with after-firing	488	105	15.7	4.7
Spark Ignition Engine 390 kWe	505	118	1.4	4.3
Spark Ignition Engine 540 kWe	453	115	1.9	4.0
HFO Diesel Engine 3.1 MWe	417	73	6.9	5.7
HFO Diesel Engine 3.1 MWe with after-firing	499	93	8.8	5.4

*   Cost expressed per kWe of installed capacity of CHP plant.

Table 5   Results of CHP Assessment at Brewery

Plant Details	Plant Capital Cost [£/kWe]*	Annual Site Running Cost Savings [£/kWe]*	Annual Site Running Cost Savings [%]	Payback Period [years]
Gas Turbine 3.0 MWe	474	106	4.5	4.5
Gas Turbine 3.0 MWe with after-firing	533	148	6.3	3.6
Gas Turbine 5.1 MWe	400	109	8.0	3.7
Gas Turbine 5.1 MWe with after-firing	444	144	10.6	3.1
Spark Ignition Engine 390 kWe	505	131	0.7	3.9
Spark Ignition Engine 540 kWe	453	127	1.0	3.6
HFO Diesel Engine 2.8 MWe	438	92	3.6	4.8
HFO Diesel Engine 2.8 MWe with after-firing	523	118	4.6	4.4
HFO Diesel Engine 3.1 MWe	417	92	4.0	4.5
HFO Diesel Engine 3.1 MWe with after-firing	499	118	5.1	4.2
Coal fired boiler - steam outlet conditions 450 psig/750°F				
Steam Turbine 3.0 MWe	1140	318	13.6	3.6
Steam Turbine 4.0 MWe	950	273	15.5	3.5
Steam Turbine 5.0 MWe	870	206	14.7	4.2

*   Cost expressed per kWe of installed capacity of CHP plant.

CHP PLANT

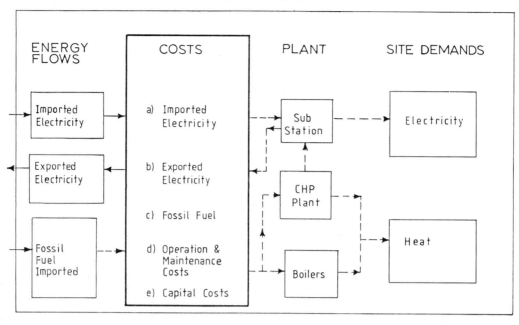

CONVENTIONAL PLANT

Fig 1   Comparison of CHP plant and conventional plant

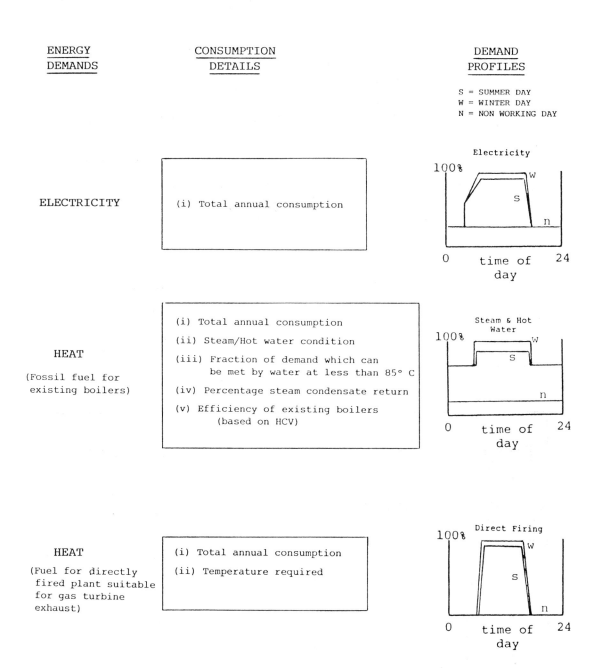

ENERGY DEMANDS	CONSUMPTION DETAILS	DEMAND PROFILES

S = SUMMER DAY
W = WINTER DAY
N = NON WORKING DAY

ELECTRICITY

(i) Total annual consumption

Electricity

HEAT

(Fossil fuel for existing boilers)

(i) Total annual consumption

(ii) Steam/Hot water condition

(iii) Fraction of demand which can be met by water at less than 85° C

(iv) Percentage steam condensate return

(v) Efficiency of existing boilers (based on HCV)

Steam & Hot Water

HEAT

(Fuel for directly fired plant suitable for gas turbine exhaust)

(i) Total annual consumption

(ii) Temperature required

Direct Firing

Fig 2   Site data requirements

75

PERFORMANCE   DATA

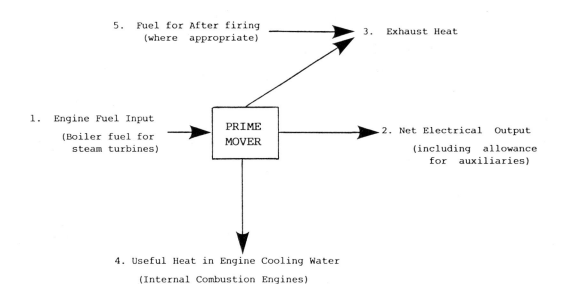

Data on performance at part load is also included

COST DATA

Capital Cost

Maintenance Cost

MAINTENANCE ALLOWANCE

Planned Maintenance

Breakdowns

Fig 3   CHP plant data requirements

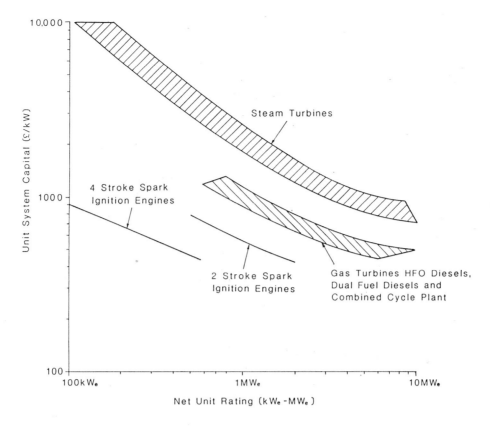

Fig 4   CHP plant installed costs (1985/86)

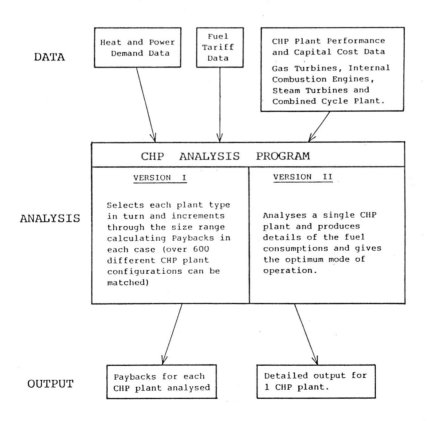

Fig 5   CHP computer program

MAX ELEC DEMAND [kW] = 15505,   MAX HEAT DEMAND (STEAM/HOT WATER) [kW] = 56181,   MAX DIRECT FIRING FUEL CONS [kW] =   0.
AVE ELEC DEMAND [kW] = 8861,   AVE HEAT DEMAND (STEAM/HOT WATER) [kW] = 32996,   AVE DIRECT FIRING FUEL CONS [kW] =   0.

PLANT TYPE	SIZE BAND CODE	NO. OF UNITS	ECONO-MIZER	AFTER-FIRED BOILER	CHP PLANT RATING [kWe]	ELEC GENERATED [MWh/YR]	ELEC EXPORTED [%]	EXISTING RUNNING COST [£/YR]	CHP PLANT CAPITAL COST [£]	NET PRESENT VALUE (10 YEAR LIFE) (5% DISC-RATE) [£]	RUNNING COST SAVING [%]	PAYBACK PERIOD [YEARS]
GAS TURBINE	3	1	1	0	2970	1.569E+04	0.0	7.017E+06	1.407E+06	1.015E+06	4.5	4.49
GAS TURBINE	3	1	1	1	2970	2.154E+04	0.0	7.017E+06	1.583E+06	1.809E+06	6.3	3.60
GAS TURBINE	3	2	1	0	2970	3.045E+04	1.4	7.017E+06	2.617E+06	2.140E+06	8.8	4.25
GAS TURBINE	3	2	1	1	2970	4.158E+04	2.1	7.017E+06	2.945E+06	3.533E+06	12.0	3.51
GAS TURBINE	3	3	1	0	2970	4.519E+04	9.3	7.017E+06	3.841E+06	3.119E+06	12.8	4.26
GAS TURBINE	3	3	1	1	2970	5.689E+04	7.3	7.017E+06	4.322E+06	4.457E+06	16.2	3.80
GAS TURBINE	4	1	1	0	5145	3.755E+04	1.5	7.017E+06	2.056E+06	2.278E+06	8.0	3.66
GAS TURBINE	4	1	1	1	5145	3.755E+04	1.5	7.017E+06	2.286E+06	3.452E+06	10.6	3.08
GAS TURBINE	4	2	1	0	5145	5.302E+04	12.5	7.017E+06	3.825E+06	4.547E+06	15.5	3.53
GAS TURBINE	4	2	1	1	5145	6.834E+04	14.6	7.017E+06	4.252E+06	5.945E+06	18.8	3.22
GAS TURBINE	4	3	1	0	5145	7.541E+04	21.9	7.017E+06	5.614E+06	6.295E+06	22.0	3.64
GAS TURBINE	4	3	1	1	5145	8.843E+04	18.7	7.017E+06	6.241E+06	7.169E+06	24.8	3.59
GAS TURBINE	5	1	1	0	2840	1.528E+04	0.0	7.017E+06	1.481E+06	6.549E+05	3.9	5.35
GAS TURBINE	5	1	1	1	2840	2.085E+04	0.0	7.017E+06	1.626E+06	1.099E+06	5.0	4.61
GAS TURBINE	5	2	1	0	2840	2.940E+04	1.0	7.017E+06	2.755E+06	1.399E+06	7.7	5.12
GAS TURBINE	5	2	1	1	2840	3.984E+04	0.7	7.017E+06	3.025E+06	2.320E+06	9.9	4.37
GAS TURBINE	5	3	1	0	2840	4.349E+04	8.1	7.017E+06	4.044E+06	2.027E+06	11.2	5.14
GAS TURBINE	5	3	1	1	2840	5.507E+04	6.3	7.017E+06	4.439E+06	3.014E+06	13.8	4.60
GAS TURBINE	6	1	1	0	3140	2.350E+04	0.0	7.017E+06	1.549E+06	1.126E+06	4.9	4.47
GAS TURBINE	6	1	1	1	3140	2.350E+04	0.0	7.017E+06	1.677E+06	1.677E+06	6.2	3.86
GAS TURBINE	6	2	1	0	3140	3.301E+04	1.9	7.017E+06	2.882E+06	2.378E+06	9.7	4.23
GAS TURBINE	6	2	1	1	3140	4.384E+04	1.4	7.017E+06	3.119E+06	3.432E+06	12.1	3.68
GAS TURBINE	6	3	1	0	3140	4.859E+04	10.5	7.017E+06	4.229E+06	3.412E+06	14.1	4.27
GAS TURBINE	6	3	1	1	3140	6.042E+04	8.4	7.017E+06	4.578E+06	4.621E+06	17.0	3.84
GAS TURBINE	7	1	1	0	3790	2.001E+04	0.0	7.017E+06	2.101E+06	1.074E+06	5.9	5.11
GAS TURBINE	7	1	1	1	3790	2.747E+04	0.0	7.017E+06	2.256E+06	1.642E+06	7.2	4.47
GAS TURBINE	7	2	1	0	3790	3.884E+04	5.3	7.017E+06	3.907E+06	2.274E+06	11.4	4.88
GAS TURBINE	7	2	1	1	3790	5.010E+04	4.1	7.017E+06	4.195E+06	3.350E+06	13.9	4.29
GAS TURBINE	7	3	1	0	3790	5.757E+04	14.6	7.017E+06	5.735E+06	3.199E+06	16.5	4.96
GAS TURBINE	7	3	1	1	3790	6.997E+04	12.0	7.017E+06	6.158E+06	4.302E+06	19.3	4.54
GAS TURBINE	8	1	1	0	4825	3.531E+04	0.8	7.017E+06	2.192E+06	2.338E+06	8.4	3.74
GAS TURBINE	8	1	1	1	4825	3.531E+04	0.8	7.017E+06	2.356E+06	2.991E+06	9.9	3.40
GAS TURBINE	8	2	1	0	4825	6.890E+04	18.6	7.017E+06	4.077E+06	4.534E+06	15.9	3.66
GAS TURBINE	8	2	1	1	4825	6.891E+04	18.6	7.017E+06	4.382E+06	5.723E+06	18.7	3.35

EXISTING FUEL COST HFO £ 2.92/GJ [HCV]
CHP PLANT FUEL COST GAS £ 2.75/GJ [HCV]

HFO DIESEL	1	1	1	0	2450	1.396E+04	0.0	7.017E+06	1.140E+06	6.038E+05	3.2	5.05
HFO DIESEL	1	1	1	1	2450	1.854E+04	0.0	7.017E+06	1.357E+06	8.871E+05	4.1	4.67
HFO DIESEL	1	2	1	0	2450	2.792E+04	4.7	7.017E+06	2.120E+06	1.201E+06	6.1	4.93
HFO DIESEL	1	2	1	1	2450	3.326E+04	2.2	7.017E+06	2.524E+06	1.761E+06	7.9	4.55
HFO DIESEL	1	3	1	0	2450	3.992E+04	6.8	7.017E+06	3.112E+06	1.569E+06	8.6	5.13
HFO DIESEL	1	3	1	1	2450	4.772E+04	6.9	7.017E+06	3.704E+06	2.403E+06	11.3	4.68
HFO DIESEL	1	1	1	0	2750	1.567E+04	0.0	7.017E+06	1.206E+06	7.489E+05	3.6	4.76
HFO DIESEL	1	1	1	1	2750	2.081E+04	0.0	7.017E+06	1.439E+06	1.074E+06	4.6	4.42
HFO DIESEL	1	2	1	0	2750	3.134E+04	6.1	7.017E+06	2.242E+06	1.422E+06	6.8	4.72
HFO DIESEL	1	2	1	1	2750	3.717E+04	3.0	7.017E+06	2.677E+06	2.076E+06	8.8	4.35
HFO DIESEL	1	3	1	0	2750	4.216E+04	4.8	7.017E+06	3.292E+06	1.795E+06	9.4	5.00
HFO DIESEL	1	3	1	1	2750	5.247E+04	8.7	7.017E+06	3.929E+06	2.769E+06	12.4	4.53
HFO DIESEL	1	1	1	0	3050	1.738E+04	0.0	7.017E+06	1.272E+06	8.940E+05	4.0	4.53
HFO DIESEL	1	1	1	1	3050	2.308E+04	0.0	7.017E+06	1.521E+06	1.262E+06	5.1	4.22
HFO DIESEL	1	2	1	0	3050	3.387E+04	5.2	7.017E+06	2.365E+06	1.643E+06	7.4	4.56
HFO DIESEL	1	2	1	1	3050	3.817E+04	4.4	7.017E+06	2.830E+06	2.404E+06	9.7	4.17

EXISTING FUEL COST HFO £ 2.92/GJ [HCV]
CHP PLANT FUEL COST HFO £ 2.92/GJ [HCV]

SPARK IGNITION	1	1	1	0	240	1.821E+03	0.0	7.017E+06	1.495E+05	9.056E+04	0.4	4.81
SPARK IGNITION	1	2	1	0	240	3.558E+03	0.0	7.017E+06	2.780E+05	1.979E+05	0.9	4.51
SPARK IGNITION	1	3	1	0	240	5.337E+03	0.0	7.017E+06	4.080E+05	2.971E+05	1.3	4.47
SPARK IGNITION	1	4	1	0	240	7.115E+03	0.0	7.017E+06	5.321E+05	4.022E+05	1.7	4.40
SPARK IGNITION	1	1	1	0	390	2.891E+03	0.0	7.017E+06	1.971E+05	1.975E+05	0.7	3.86
SPARK IGNITION	1	2	1	0	390	5.781E+03	0.0	7.017E+06	3.666E+05	4.067E+05	1.4	3.66
SPARK IGNITION	1	3	1	0	390	8.672E+03	0.0	7.017E+06	5.380E+05	6.132E+05	2.1	3.61
SPARK IGNITION	1	4	1	0	390	1.156E+04	0.0	7.017E+06	7.016E+05	8.275E+05	2.8	3.54
SPARK IGNITION	1	1	1	0	540	4.002E+03	0.0	7.017E+06	2.447E+05	2.831E+05	1.0	3.58

EXISTING FUEL COST HFO £ 2.92/GJ [HCV]
CHP PLANT FUEL COST GAS £ 2.75/GJ [HCV]

OVE ARUP AND PARTNERS

Fig 6   Sample printout from computer program — version I

```
                    SITE IS   BREWERY        (BAND 3 )
                    ********************

MAXIMUM DEMANDS-   ELEC = 15505.kW  HEAT = 56181.kW  DIRECT FIRE =      0.kW
DAILY AVE DEMANDS- ELEC =  8861.kW  HEAT = 32996.kW  DIRECT FIRE =      0.kW
EFFICIENCY OF EXISTING BOILERS 77.0%

PLANT IS  HFO DIESEL      NO OF UNITS = 1        UNIT RATING =  3300 KW
SIZE BAND CODE  1         BOILER ECONOMISER = 1  FIRED BOILER = 0

  EXISTING FUEL COST HFO  £  2.92/GJ [HCV]
  CHP PLANT FUEL COST HFO  £  2.92/GJ [HCV]


                                       CHP            EXISTING SYSTEM
TOTAL ANNUAL RUNNING COST         £ 6714863.           £ 7016895.

CHP FUEL COST                     £  557865.           £        0.
FOSSIL FUEL COST (EXISTING PLANT) £ 3731356.           £ 3946052.
ELEC IMPORT COST   UNIT CHARGES,  £ 1851095.           £ 2521281.
ELEC EXPORT CREDIT (UNIT CREDITS) £    3713.           £        0.
ELEC MAX DEMAND CHARGES,          £  322270.           £  409403.
ELEC STANDING CHARGES             £  140350.           £  140160.
ANNUAL MAINTENANCE COST (PLANNED) £   94031.           £        0.
MAX DEMAND BREAKDOWN PENALTY      £   21609.

TOTAL ANNUAL CHP FUEL                1811.  kTh            0.  kTh
TOTAL FOSSIL FUEL (EXISTING PLANT)  12112.  kTh        12809.  kTh
TOTAL ELEC IMPORT                   58955.  MWH        77623.  MWH
TOTAL ELEC EXPORT                     138.  MWH            0.  MWH
TOTAL ELEC GENERATED                18806.  MWH            0.  MWH
MACHINE RUNNING HOURS PER YEAR       5698.


     CAPITAL COST                 £ 1326357.
     NET ANNUAL COST SAVINGS      £  302033.
     SIMPLE PAYBACK PERIOD            4.391 YEARS

     PRIMARY ENERGY SAVING                        4015. TCE/YR
     NET PRESENT VALUE (30%Discount-Rate,10Yr Life) £ -392473.
     NET PRESENT VALUE (10%Discount-Rate,10Yr Life) £  528123.
     NET PRESENT VALUE (5% Discount-Rate,10Yr Life) £ 1005334.

              MATCHING         (1=ELEC 2=HEAT 3=SWITCH OFF)
              *******

                                       *** PERIOD ***
                      NO. DAYS    NIGHT      DAY     EVENING
DAY TYPE WINTER          74        3.        2.        2.
         WINTER/SPRING   51        3.        2.        2.
         SPRING/SUMMER   77        3.        2.        2.
         SUMMER         101        3.        2.        2.
         NONWORKING,     62        3.        2.        2.


                              OVE ARUP AND PARTNERS
```

Fig 7   Sample printout from computer program — version II
(Heavy fuel oil diesel engine without after-firing)

```
                    SITE IS   BREWERY        (BAND 3 )
                    *********************

MAXIMUM DEMANDS-  ELEC = 15505.kW   HEAT = 56181.kW   DIRECT FIRE =     0.kW
DAILY AVE DEMANDS- ELEC =  8861.kW  HEAT = 32996.kW   DIRECT FIRE =     0.kW
EFFICIENCY OF EXISTING BOILERS 77.0%

PLANT IS HFO DIESEL      NO OF UNITS = 1        UNIT RATING =   3300 KW
SIZE BAND CODE  1        BOILER ECONOMISER = 1  FIRED BOILER = 1

  EXISTING FUEL COST HFO  £  2.92/GJ [HCV]
  CHP PLANT FUEL COST HFO  £  2.92/GJ [HCV]


                                          CHP          EXISTING SYSTEM
TOTAL ANNUAL RUNNING COST          £ 6628311.          £ 7016895.

CHP FUEL COST                      £ 1414232.          £        0.
FOSSIL FUEL COST (EXISTING PLANT)  £ 2861244.          £ 3946052.
ELEC IMPORT COST    UNIT CHARGES,  £ 1745956.          £ 2521281.
ELEC EXPORT CREDIT (UNIT CREDITS)  £    3063.          £        0.
ELEC MAX DEMAND CHARGES,           £  322270.          £   409403.
ELEC STANDING CHARGES              £  140350.          £   140160.
ANNUAL MAINTENANCE COST (PLANNED)  £  124871.          £        0.
MAX DEMAND BREAKDOWN PENALTY       £   22453.

TOTAL ANNUAL CHP FUEL                4591.  kTh          0.   kTh
TOTAL FOSSIL FUEL (EXISTING PLANT)   9288.  kTh      12809.   kTh
TOTAL ELEC IMPORT                   52763.  MWH      77623.   MWH
TOTAL ELEC EXPORT                     114.  MWH          0.   MWH
TOTAL ELEC GENERATED                24974.  MWH          0.   MWH
MACHINE RUNNING HOURS PER YEAR       7567.


        CAPITAL COST              £ 1589867.
        NET ANNUAL COST SAVINGS   £  388585.
        SIMPLE PAYBACK PERIOD          4.091 YEARS

        PRIMARY ENERGY SAVING                        6995. TCE/YR
        NET PRESENT VALUE (30%Discount-Rate,10Yr Life) £ -388364.
        NET PRESENT VALUE (10%Discount-Rate,10Yr Life) £  796042.
        NET PRESENT VALUE (5% Discount-Rate,10Yr Life) £ 1410005.

                    MATCHING      (1=ELEC 2=HEAT 3=SWITCH OFF)
                    ********

                                          *** PERIOD ***
                        NO. DAYS    NIGHT      DAY       EVENING
DAY TYPE WINTER           74          2.        2.         2.
         WINTER/SPRING    51          2.        2.         2.
         SPRING/SUMMER    77          2.        2.         2.
         SUMMER          101          2.        2.         2.
         NONWORKING,      62          3.        2.         2.


                                          OVE ARUP AND PARTNERS
```

Fig 8   Sample printout from computer program — version II
(Heavy fuel oil diesel engine with after-firing)

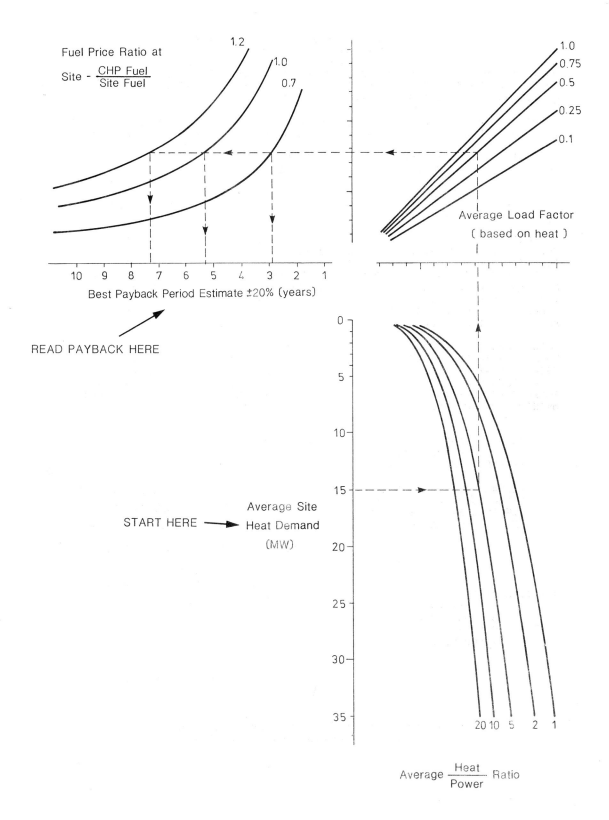

Fig 9   Preliminary CHP assessment chart — gas turbine plant

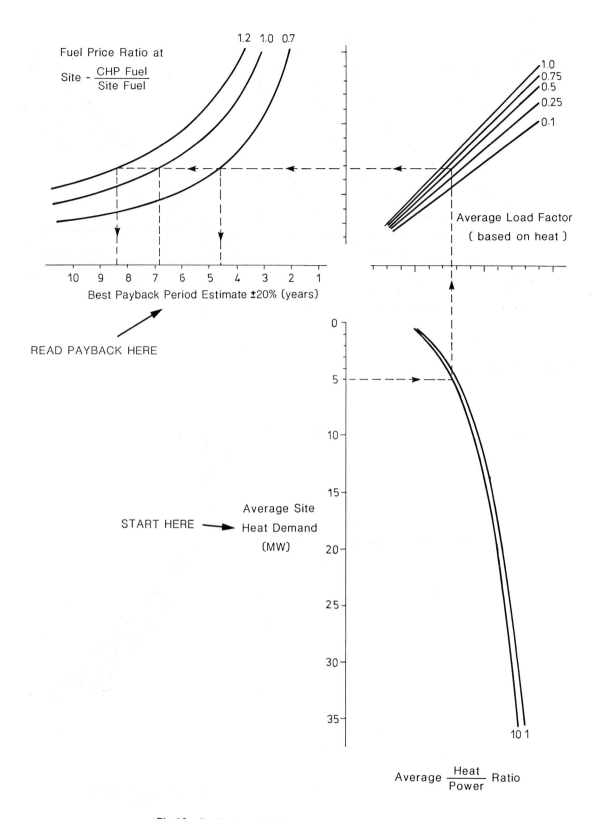

Fuel Price Ratio at

Site - $\dfrac{\text{CHP Fuel}}{\text{Site Fuel}}$

1.2 1.0 0.7

Best Payback Period Estimate ±20% (years)

READ PAYBACK HERE

1.0
0.75
0.5
0.25
0.1

Average Load Factor
(based on heat)

START HERE ⟶ Average Site
Heat Demand
(MW)

Average $\dfrac{\text{Heat}}{\text{Power}}$ Ratio

Fig 10   Preliminary CHP assessment chart — spark ignition
engine plant

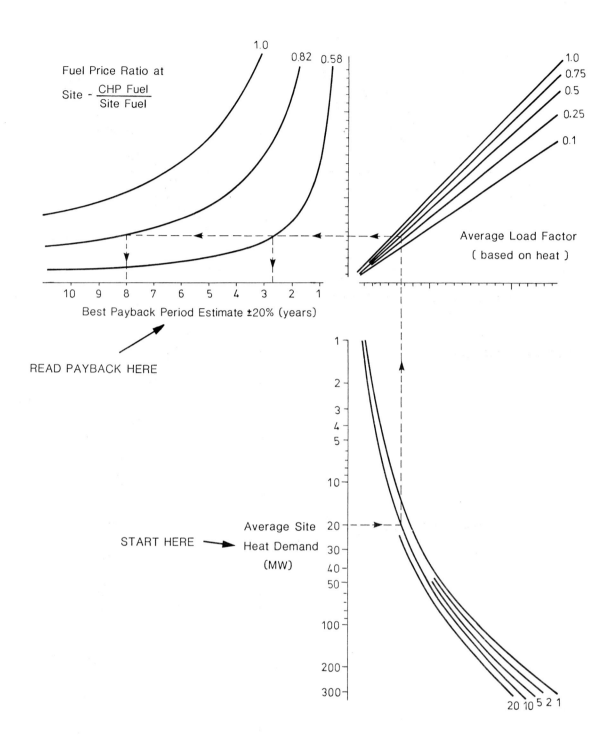

Fig 11   Preliminary CHP assessment chart — coal fired
boiler/steam turbine plant

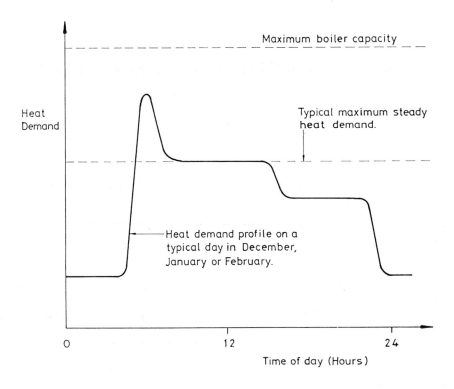

Fig 12   Definition of Typical Maximum Steady Heat Demand

Small-scale co-generation in a papermill

A McBAY, TEng, MIPlantE
Gestetner Papers Ltd

SYNOPSIS   Expensive energy means its efficient and cost effective use is becoming increasingly important and co-generation, even on a small scale, is one way in which continuous process industries can make savings.   This paper details one such application in a papermill, where various energy saving options were examined in conjunction with projected savings and factors which affect process performance.   The resulting installation and its performance are outlined.

1   INTRODUCTION

J.A. Weir Ltd.,(formerly Gestetner Papers Ltd.), a wholly-owned subsidiary of Gestetner Holdings, is a medium-sized 38,000 tonnes per year papermill situated on a 50 acre site in Central Scotland.   Some 295 people are employed in the converting and manufacturing of woodfree offset, copier, stencil, cash roll and listing papers.

The site has housed papermachines since 1974 and today has two fully computerised papermachines which, since January 1985, operate 6,500 hours per year on a continuous 5-shift system.

Papermaking operations (Figure 1) consist essentially of forming a wet web of paper on a plastic forming fabric, pressing it to reduce its moisture to a level sufficient to render it capable of being strong enough to pass over 60 inch diameter steam heated drying cylinders, of which there are 45 on one of the machines installed at J.A. Weir.

2   ELECTRICITY AND STEAM SERVICES

For many years steam was produced by four 20,000 lb/h (at operating temperature and pressure) coal fired water-tube boilers at a pressure of 275 lb/in^2 which fed a 3MW pass-out condensing turbo-alternator set.   Operation of the condensing turbine became less viable with age and as the electricity supply from the South of Scotland Electricity Board become more reliable and, in real terms, lower in cost.   A 500 bhp Allen CF4G single-stage back-pressure turbine had been installed in 1967 as the prime mover for the No.4 papermachine.   This was successful and when the time came for the coal-fired boilers to be replaced, new boilers operating at steam conditions suitable for the turbine inlet were purchased. The new boilers (Figure 2) were three oil-fired Parkinson Cowan GWB wet-back shell boilers, each operating at 240 lb/in^2 (G) and 460°F (on oil firing) and capable of 30,000 lb/h (from and at 212°F), in the region of the limit of shell boiler output at that time.

A superheater is fitted into the reversal chamber between the first and second pass of the boiler gas path and is exposed to both convective and radiant heat.   This means operational care is required when starting up the boilers to avoid possibility of superheater over-heating and failure.

Oil was chosen as the fuel because of two factors(1) reduced capital cost of the boiler plant and(2) essential requirement in the paper process of fast response to dramatic load change which occurs when the paper web breaks and is restarted.

In 1981 another Allen single-stage turbine was installed (Figure 3), in conjunction with rebuilding papermachine No.4 to enable it to operate at higher speeds and give greater output.   At the same time the boilers were converted to burn natural gas which, through a two-year, 100-day interruptible gas contract, achieved maximum savings.   Heavy fuel oil was retained as the standby fuel.   As a safeguard the boiler tubes were trepanned to avoid the possibility of tube-end splits to which these boilers are susceptible on conversion to gas firing.

Figure 4 shows the distribution diagram for the mill's steam services.   High-pressure steam raised at 240 lb/in^2 and 600°F (gas firing) is passed directly to two users, the 600 bhp turbine driving PM4 and a thermo-chemical starch cooker which have a combined steam requirement of approximately 21,000 lb/h.   The rest of the steam, between 19,000 and 35,000 lb/h according to the time of year, was passed through a combined de-super-heater and pressure-reducing valve to reduce it to the low-pressure distribution main requirement of 25 to 32 lb/in^2 mainly being used with the turbine exhaust in the drying sections of the papermachines.

3   DEVELOPMENT OF SERVICES

At that time all electricity was bought in from the SSEB, at 11 kV and fed to a main switchboard for distribution to various parts of the mill. One feeder was connected to 11,500 kVA transformer which supplied a 440V switchboard situated in the old power station, Figure 5.   In 1982 a maximum demand of 3875 kVA was recorded when importing approximately 17.7 GW hr.

This prompted the company to commission a technical and economic analysis of schemes for the more efficient use of steam required for process resulting in two existing options and one future option being considered.

Option 1:

To refurbish the retained ex-PM4 prime-mover 500 bhp Allen turbine to drive papermachine No.5 which was being driven by a 214.7 hp Harland PMA electric motor.

Option 2:

To use all the available steam, other than that required to supply the papermachine No.4 prime-mover turbine and thermo-chemical starch cooker to drive a new turbo-alternator and to exhaust the steam into the low-pressure ring main at 25 to 32 lb/in^2.

Future Option:

It was recognised that at some time in the future the existing boilers would need replacing. If new boilers produced steam at a higher pressure and temperature than at present this steam could power a _more efficient_ but standard low-cost type of multi-stage turbine to drive a higher output alternator. Under these circumstances it may well be economic to replace the PM4 turbine drive by an electric motor to maximise steam utilisation through the larger turbo-alternator.

4   EQUIPMENT REQUIREMENTS

The requirements of the various options were examined in detail in conjunction with plant and equipment manufacturers, and assessed as follows.

Option 1:

The 500 bhp turbine (ex PM4 prime-mover) could be refurbished with new nozzles, gear and governor to drive PM5. This would require 8,350 lb/hr at 210 lb/in^2 of steam to produce 204 bhp at 2,500 r/min., leaving approximately 7,000 lb/h of steam in Summer and 24,000 lb/h in Winter passing through the pressure-reducing and de-superheating stations.

Option 2:

The maximum steam available for the new turbo-alternator, if the turbine drive for PM4 and electric motor drive on PM5 remained, would be a minimum of 19,000 lb/h in the Summer and a maximum of 35,000 lb/h in the Winter (Figure 6). This was too high a flow for the 500 bhp turbine (ex PM4 prime-mover) to accommodate, even with modification, and a new turbine would be required which it was estimated would produce an average of around 700 kW in the Winter and 500 kW in the Summer (Figure 7).

Future Option:

On the basis of using steam at, say, 450 lb/in^2 and 700°F it would be possible to generate some 2,600 kW in Winter and 1,400 kW in Summer from flows of 58,600 and 38,700 lb/h respectively, using an Allen type SLC multi-stage turbo-alternator.

The de-aerators necessary for the high pressure boilers would require steam, so giving the higher steam flows available for the turbine.

The boilers would be water-tube design and as such would be more efficient than shell type. They would however be more expensive. Either high-pressure water-tube or shell-type boilers operating at the present pressure could be coal-fired if coal prices in the future, and grants for conversion, justify it.

At the time it was considered that it would probably not be worthwhile purchasing a more expensive boiler and turbine operating at a higher pressure than 450 lb/in^2 to produce the mill's maximum demand of about 3,600 kW. However, enactment of the Energy Act in 1985, allowing the possibility of worthwhile power export, makes this worth considering in the future.

5   ECONOMIC ANALYSIS

The operational effects and economic benefit of installing Options 1 and 2 were assessed, and indicated that operational savings of £18,000 per annum and £56,000 per annum to give simple paybacks of 2.5 and 2 years respectively. The analyses did not cater for interest on capital, corporation tax or government grants, and were based on the mill running 132 hours per week for 48 weeks per year.

Option 2 was clearly the most advantageous and the method of assessment is detailed as follows

From information indicated in Figure 6 and Figure 7 it was predicted that:

Ave. generator load in Winter = 700 kWe at mechanical efficiency 0.89

Ave. generator load in Summer = 500 kWe at mechanical efficiency 0.86

Overall savings were calculated:

(a) _Actual (1982) Electrical Costs based on Annual Maximum Demand (AMD) Tariff with all power from SSEB_

Supply Capacity	3950 kVA
Basic Demand	3920 kVA
Peak Demand	3875 kVA

Peak Demand

For each kVA of Maximum Demand during prescribed hours in the three months mainly within the period December to February inclusive, in each year of supply.

The prescribed hours are - 0730 to 0900
                            1330 to 1530
                            1700 to 2130

Basic Demand Charge

For the kVA of Maximum Demand at any time in each year of supply. (kVA of Maximum Demand means twice the greatest number of kilovolt ampere hours and when during any thirty consecutive minutes.)

Day Units   11,158,800 (Winter Day 4,875,900 +)
                       (Summer Day 6,282,900   )

Night Units 6,502,900

3,950 kVA @ £ 5.29/kVA = £20,895.50
3,875 kVA @ £12.49/kVA = £48,398.75
1,000 kVA @ £21.12/kVA = £21,120.00
2,920 kVA @ £11.35/kVA = £33,142.00

4,875,900 kWh @ 3.74p/kWh = £182,358.66
6,282,900 kWh @ 2.33p/kWh = £146,391.57
6,502,900 kWh @ 1.85p/kWh = £120,303.65

TOTAL COST = £572,610.13 PER YEAR

(b) _Future Electricity Costs, AMD Tariff (1983/ 1984) All Power from SSEB_

An estimated increase in tariff in April 1983 of 5 per cent was assumed.

Supply Capacity   3950 kVA
Basic Demand   3920 kVA
Peak Demand   3875 kVA
Day Units   11,158,800
(Winter Day 4,875,900 + Summer Day 6,282,900)
Night Units   6,502,900

9,950kVA @ £ 5.55/kVA = £21,923
3,875kVA @ £13.11/kVA = £50,801
1,000kVA @ £22.18/kVA = £22,180
2,920kVA @ £11.92/kVA = £35,164

4,875,900 kWh @ £3.93p/kWh = £191,623
6,282,900 kWh @ £2.45p/kWh = £153,931
6,502,900 kWh @ £1.95p/kWh = £126,156

TOTAL COST = £601,240 PER YEAR

(c) Future Electricity Costs (1983/84) with Co-Generation (AMD Tariff Terms with Standby Capacity

Assuming generator output of 700 kW in the Winter and 500 kW in the Summer, corresponding to mean Winter and Summer turbine steam through-puts of 31,500 and 23,000 lb/h respectively.

It should be noted that the steam requirement in the Winter period was assessed as 24 operating weeks per year, whereas the electrical tariff Winter period covered 19 operational weeks. An integral part of AMD tariff includes a capacity charge equivalent to the full utilisation of the existing supply capacity as a maximum demand against the AMD tariff.

Supply Capacity   3950 kVA
Basic Demand   3950 kVA
Peak Demand   3950 kVA

Winter Day Units = 4,875,900
                  - 19 x 132 x 700 x 0.632
                  = 3,766,361

Summer Day Units = 6,282,900
                  - (5x132x700)+ (24x132x500) x
                    0.632
                  = 4,982,828

Night Units   = 6,502,900
                  - (24x132x700)+ (24x132x500) x
                    0.368
                  = 5,103,911

Supply Capacity 3950kVA @ £ 5.55/kVA = £21,923
Peak Demand   3950kVA @ £13.11/kVA = £51,785
Basic Demand   1000kVA @ £22.18/kVA = £22,180
                2950kVA @ £11.92/kVA = £35,164

     3,766,361kWh @ 3.93p/kWh = £148,018
     4,989,828kWh @ 2.45p/kWh = £122,251
     5,103,911kWh @ 1.95p/kWh = £ 99,016

TOTAL COST = £369,285 + £131,051 = £500,336

.˙. Savings in imported electricity charges
  = (b) - (c) = £601,240 - 500,336
              = £100,904 per annum

Calculations against different tariffs showed that Annual Maximum Tariff still held financial advantages over Monthly Maximum Demand Tariff, and the Annual Maximum Demand Tariff was retained.

(d) Additional Cost associated with Co-Generation

There are additional costs arising from extra gas usage to offset the energy taken from the steam to produce electricity, as it passes through the turbine. Since the pressure and temperature of the steam leaving the boiler is unchanged, in practice the difference is an increase in mass flow corresponding to a reduction in the quantity of water injected into the de-super-

heater to achieve the desired steam conditions at points of low-pressure usage. However, the easiest way to calculate additional costs is from energy extracted as electricity.

Gas Costs = 24.63p/therm
1 therm per hour = 29.3 kWh
.˙. Gas Costs = £0.0084/kWh
Cost of raising additional steam

$$= \frac{\text{Electricity (kW)}}{\text{T/alt effy. x boiler effy.}} \times \text{Gas Cost in £/kW x time (hours)}$$

.˙. Additional Steam Cost (Winter)

$$= \frac{700}{0.89 \times 0.80} \times 0.0084 \times 132 \times 24$$

= £26,163

Additional Steam Cost (Summer)

$$= \frac{500}{0.86 \times 0.80} \times 0.0084 \times 132 \times 24$$

= £19,339

.˙. Total Additional Steam Cost = £45,502 p.a.

.˙. Nett Savings

= Electrical Savings - Additional Steam Cost

= £100,904 - £45,502

= £ 55,402 Per Annum

(e) Project Cost Estimate

An Allen type SSK5GD integrally geared single-stage steam turbine coupled to an 830 kW alternator complete with electrical control

Package   .. ..   £ 95,670
415V cabling ex-alternator/CB/HT
  transformer .. ..   £ 2,895
Piping, valves, insulation, services £ 8,861
Commission charges   ..   .. ..   £ 1,700
Civil Works .. ..   £ 1,400
Contingency .. ..   £ 5,000
                                      ────────
                                      £115,526

Simple return on investment = $\dfrac{£115,526}{£ 55,402}$

  = approximately 2 years

6   PLANT AND OPERATION

Having considered the options and decided to follow the private generation route, the mill consulted the South of Scotland Electricity Board (SSEB) at an early stage to obtain the necessary permission to parallel with the Board's system, and to ensure that the proposals met with Engineering Recommendations G26 of the Electricity Council governing the installed and operational aspects of private generating plant.

The mill was fortunate with regard to siting for the proposed turbo-alternator unit, because the space previously occupied by an old 3MW pass-out and condensing turbine was available alongside the low-pressure main and pressure-reducing station, so the civil work for foundations was less than would otherwise have been the case.

There also existed a hand-operated overhead travelling crane immediately above the site of the old 3MW turbo-alternator set.

It was essential that the turbo-alternator (Figure 8) would run unattended, except for hourly logging of pressures and other data, and reparalleling when necessary, and the design therefore had to cater for automated operation.

(a) Operating Philosophy

An operating philosophy and specification for the turbo-alternator set was drawn up in conjunction with W.H. Allen to cover the generation of 440V electrical power being fed into the existing Reyrolle-Belmos switchboard in the turbine house via an extension to the panel (Figure 9) which accommodates all the turbine and alternator controls.

Figure 10, the electrical distribution diagram, shows the arrangement for the turbo-alternator set via the 1500kVA transformer (No.5). There are two 11kV SSEB feeders and total failure rarely occurs.

When operating in parallel with the SSEB supply the turbo-alternator is under the control of a back-pressure regulator so that all process steam passes through the turbine, and generated power is dependent upon the process steam demand.

In the event of failure of the SSEB supply the turbo-alternator will continue to supply the connected electrical load (which includes the boilerhouse services) under speed control, and the steam passing through the turbine will depend on the electrical load connected. It is expected that this would result in a rise in pressure on the exhaust, and excess steam would therefore be discharged through the system relief valve. Maintaining the electrical supply to the boilerhouse is expected to be on a temporary basis, to allow an operator to decide on further action depending on whether the SSEB supply loss is likely to be of short or long duration.

If the SSEB supply to transformer No.5 fails the associated 440 volt circuit breaker in the switchboard would trip automatically, and an auxiliary switch on the circuit breaker would change the mode of operation from back-pressure control to speed control. On recovery of the SSEB supply an operator would trip the alternator circuit breaker, close the transformer LV breaker and resynchronise the turbo-alternator, so resuming parallel operation. An interlock system ensures that the act of closing the transformer LV breaker can only be achieved if the alternator circuit breaker is open in order to prevent accidental synchronising out-of-phase. Intertripping between the transformer LV and HV breakers is not closed when the HV breaker is open.

Since the total load on the power station switchboard does not normally exceed 1000 amps it is probable that, at times, power would be exported through transformer No.5 into the mill's 11kV system. In these circumstances it is not possible to detect loss of the SSEB supply by means of the reverse power relay. It is essential to trip the transformer LV breaker but leaving all 11 kV breakers closed in anticipation of resumption of the SSEB supply. Loss of SSEB supply would result in the total mill load being carried by the turbo-alternator. This situation will be detected by a time-delayed under-voltage relay to trip the transformer LV breaker. If the turbo-alternator cannot supply all the load connected to the switchboard it will slow down through overload and an underfrequency relay will trip the pulp refinery supply circuit breaker, allowing the speed to recover.

The switchboard extension panel incorporates sufficient instrumentation to enable operation under manual control, although operation is normally automatic with watch-keeping attendance only. Automatic protection facilities are provided for mechanical and electrical faults, and the installation complies with Engineering Recommendations G26 and has been approved by the SSEB.

(b) Turbine Controls

The Allen turbine is equipped with a speed governor, for start-up and single operation, fitted with a speeder motor to facilitate synchronising. After synchronising the speed governor is overridden by the back-pressure regulator (Figure 11) which maintains exhaust pressure. On disconnecting the alternator from parallel operation the turbine reverts to speed control.

The turbine is also fitted with:
Solenoid trip valve to enable it to be shut down from a remote point or automatically (energise to trip).

Local push-button for emergency trip.

Low lubricating oil pressure alarm and trip, via pressure switches and trip solenoid valve, for turbine and gearbox.

High lubricating oil temperature alarm and trip via contact thermometer and relay.

Solenoid valve for automatic changeover from back-pressure to speed control (energise to speed control).

Standard instruments normal for this type of operation.

(c) Alternator

The alternator decided upon was a Peebles brushless screen protected foot-mounted machine (Figure 12) rated at 835 kW 1043.75 kVA, 0.8 power factor, 440 volts, 3-phase, 4-wire, 50H$_z$ at 1500 r/min complete with the following features and accessories:

Terminal box for eleven 240mm^2 single-core cables.

Automatic voltage regulator with motorised voltage setting potentiometer.

Anti-condensation heater.

Power factor regulator to maintain generated power-factor at any preset level between 0.8 and unit when in parallel with SSEB.

7   EXPERIENCE TO DATE

Since commissioning, the mill has changed its operations from 3-shift 134 hours per week to 5-shift 168 hours per week, which should have increased the electrical units produced and thus the economic viability.

In practice the cost of gas to produce additional steam has proved less than calculated. This would indicate that either the boilers and/or turbine are more efficient than originally estimated, that steam loads are less than expected, or, even though normally shut, that the combined pressure-reducing and de-superheating valve bypassing the turbine leaks, or a combination of all three.

That lower gas usage occurred in conjunction with fewer units being generated than anticipated during this first period of monitored operation showed that the first condition is not responsible to any significant degree. Discrepancies have been traced to leakage through the pressure-reducing valve which has been overcome by closing the upstream manually operated isolator valve, and there is a higher than expected pressure drop in the steam supply to the turbine, which is operating at off-design conditions.

When a papermachine has a paper break and re-starts after threading up there is a sudden additional short term steam demand of up to 15,000 lb/h with a corresponding fall in back-pressure in the L.P. steam main. If the turbine is running with the secondary nozzles open and if this occurs the turbine can provide a greater than designed transient output which can and usually does cause a trip. To avoid this happening frequently the turbine is often run with the secondary nozzles shut which gives a typical winter load loss of circa 100 kW.

To overcome this an electrical load limiter system is being designed and installed. It will consist of a kW transducer connected in series with the current transformers in the load indicator in the turbine control board to give a 4-20 mA signal which will be proportional to load. (Figure 13)

This signal will be fed to an additional current to pneumatic (I/P) pressure controller with a 3-15 psi output which will fall with rise in electrical load. It will be combined with the output of the existing pneumatic back-pressure controller through a signal selector which will prohibit the back-pressure controller from increasing electrical load beyond the set point on the electrical load controller, i.e. the I/P controller.

A 4-20 mA electrical load indicator will be connected in series with the I/P controller and will be mounted in the field beside the I/P controller. The generator to date has produced some 6×10^6 kWh and has run without any notable engineering or electrical problems.

8   OBSERVATIONS

The introduction of the 1983 Energy Act made possibilities for private generation more viable in that the various Electricity Boards must co-operate fully with potential chp operators. This co-operation is essential in the provision of standby power at a reasonable cost, which if not forthcoming can wreck the economics of small-scale chp schemes.

Annual Maximum Demand Tariffs are offered by most Electricity Boards which incorporate immediate penalty costs in the event of chp generator failure if this tariff is used. Some Electricity Boards will insist that chp user's supply capacity, peak demand and basic demand capacities remain unchanged after a chp installation. It would be more advantageous to industry if these Electricity Boards were to be more flexible in the application of tariffs, possibly offering one based on unit charges alone. Perhaps evolution of the 1983 Energy Act will encourage Electricity Boards to approach tariffs for chp co-generators more flexibly.

ACKNOWLEDGEMENTS

The author would like to thank the Directors of J.A. Weir Ltd. for permission to publish this paper, and to Mr. F. Nash of NEI-APE Ltd. and the Commercial Office of SSEB, Falkirk who have contributed to its preparation.

Fig 1 Front view of No. 4 Papermachine showing 60 inch diameter steam dryers

Fig 2 Three Parkinson Cowan GWB Model 875 boilers

Fig 3 PM4 prime-mover turbine 600 HP

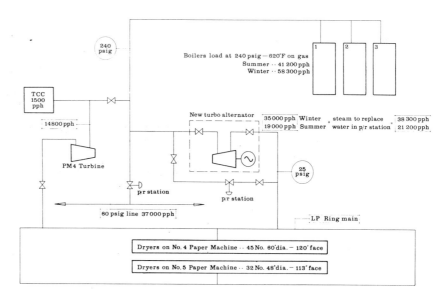

Fig 4 Mill steam distribution diagram

Fig 5   Extension to existing mill 440 V switchboard

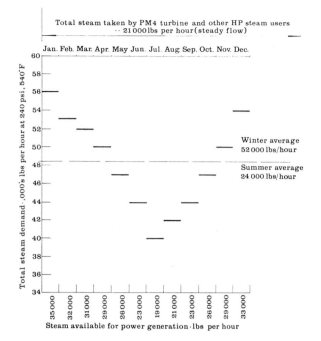

Fig 6   Graph showing seasonal availability for LP steam for turbo-alternator

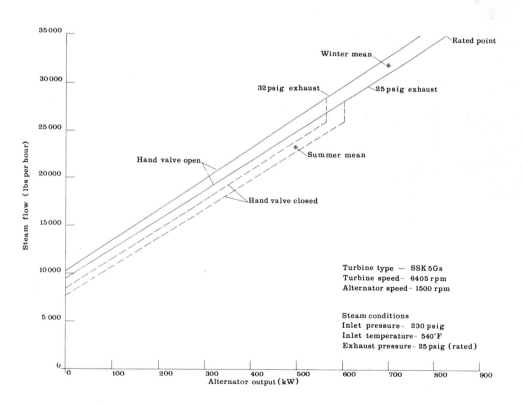

Fig 7   Graph of steam flow versus kilowatts turbo-alternator

Fig 8   Allen type SSK5GD x 830 kW turbo-alternator

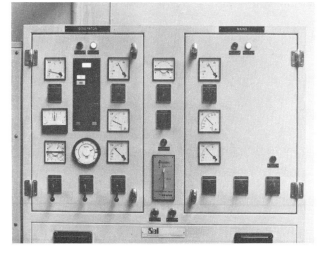

Fig 9   Turbo-alternator control panel

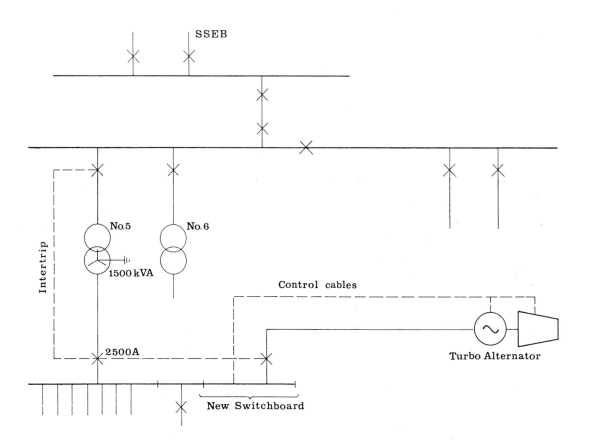

Fig 10   Mill electrical distribution diagram

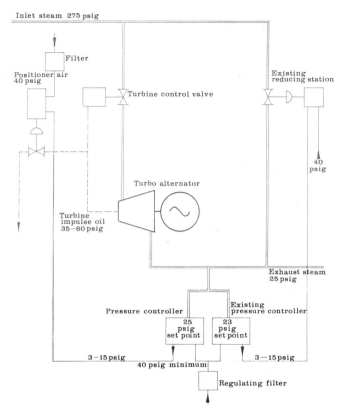

Inlet steam 275 psig

Filter

Positioner air
40 psig

Turbine control valve

Existing
reducing station

40
psig

Turbo alternator

Turbine
impulse oil
35–60 psig

Exhaust steam
25 psig

Pressure controller

Existing
pressure controller

25
psig
set point

23
psig
set point

3–15 psig

3–15 psig

40 psig minimum

Regulating filter

Fig 11   Diagramatic layout of back-pressure control loops

Fig 12   Peebles brushless alternator 835 kW x 1043.75 kVA

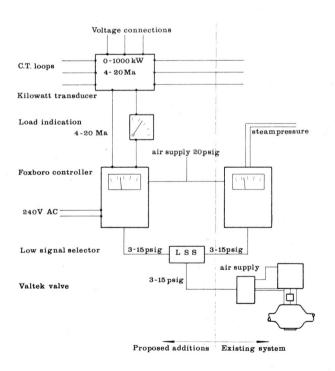

Voltage connections

C.T. loops

0-1000 kW
4- 20 Ma

Kilowatt transducer

Load indication
4-20 Ma

steam pressure

air supply 20 psig

Foxboro controller

240V AC

Low signal selector

3-15 psig   L S S   3-15 psig

Valtek valve

3-15 psig

air supply

Proposed additions   Existing system

Fig 13   Diagramatic layout of electrical load limiter system

Commercial arrangements for co-generation in the UK and USA

D L TOLLEY, BSc(Eng), MBA and **G J FOWLER**, BSc(Eng)
The Electricity Council

SYNOPSIS The impact of the PURPA legislation in the US and the Energy Act 1983 in the UK on the nature of the purchase tariffs for cogenerators and CHP plant is examined, and reasons considered why the prospects for investment by private generators might be enhanced in the United States.

1   INTRODUCTION

The past few years have seen changes in policies towards the competitive environment for electricity supply in both the US and UK. In both countries Governments have sought to introduce competition into electricity supply by removing institutional and legal barriers. The objective has been to promote the efficient use of energy, and thus its conservation by ensuring that economic schemes for electricity generation, especially those that encompass the commercial use of heat (cogeneration or CHP) are not overlooked. The legislation that has backed this change of policy is the Public Utilities Regulatory Policies Act (PURPA) in the US, and the Energy Act 1983 in the UK. These statutory instruments display some remarkable similarities but it is sometimes suggested that whereas PURPA has stimulated a significant growth in privately operated CHP plant, there has been no parallel development in the UK. This paper compares the basis for the commercial arrangements in each country before looking at the possible reasons for this claim.

2   UK LEGISLATION

Prior to the 1983 Energy Act any company, person or other body was legally entitled to install generating plant to meet his own needs. Furthermore any company or person, but not a Local Authority, could sell electricity to a third party provided this did not become his main business. This restriction gave electricity supply authorities a so called statutory monopoly; a situation which has existed since 1909. In seeking to encourage the generation and supply of electricity by private persons or companies the initial provision of the Energy Act removes this monopoly. The position has been emphasised by the objectives given to the Chairmen of the Electricity Council and CEGB by the Secretary of State for Energy and which require them to increase the scope for competition.

The early part of the Act places a requirement on all Boards to make an offer, unless technically impractical, following a request from a private generator to:

(i)   supply him with electricity either for his own use or that of his customers;

(ii)   purchase electricity generated by him; and

(iii) allow him to use the Boards' transmission and distribution system.

In addition tariffs must be published for each situation by all Boards although the CEGB is not obliged to publish a tariff for the purchase of privately generated electricity. The setting of tariffs is the responsibility of each Board, but the Act also requires that there should be consultation between both the Board and the Electricity Council, and the Electricity Council and the Secretary of State on the Methods and Principles on which the tariffs are framed.

Whilst the methods and principles are, in the first instance, a matter for the electricity supply industry (esi), the Energy Act indicates some of the more fundamental axioms on which the tariffs must be based. In the case of purchases the tariff must:-

(a)   not increase the prices paid by other customers of the Board as a result of the purchase; and

(b)   reflect the costs that would have been borne by the Board but for the purchase.

The choice of a Board's avoided cost, rather than those of the Industry, is a deliberate political decision and leads to considerable transparency in the purchase tariff since over three quarters of an Area Board's total costs derive from the published Bulk Supply Tariff (BST) under which the Area Board purchases its supplies from the CEGB.

For the use of system tariff the Act requires that the Board should identify a path through the system between the private generator and his consumer along which a hypothetical flow of power can occur. The Board is then empowered to seek a return on the relevant assets in this path that is "comparable to any return that the Board expects to receive on comparable assets."

3 US LEGISLATION

PURPA was enacted in November 1978 as one of the five pieces of legislation that comprise the National Energy Act. It contains two sections that condition the commercial arrangements between a cogenerator and the host utility. Section 210 requires a utility to sell electricity to, and purchase electricity from qualifying facilities (QFs). In turn, section 201 defines a QF as either a cogeneration plant (where a minimum of 5% of the input energy must be available as heat for commercial use) or a small power producer (which is one not larger than 80MW and which uses biomass, waste or renewable resources as a primary energy source).

Section 210 also empowers the Federal Energy Regulatory Commission (FERC) to determine rate guidelines for the utility's purchases. But in making this provision Congress directed that the rules be based on the "incremental cost to the electric utility of alternative electric energy". Accordingly, FERC decided that the rates paid to QFs would be considered to comply with PURPA if they were set equal to the costs the utility avoids by not having to supply electricity from its own resources. This approach based on marginal cost principles was specifically chosen, and subsequently upheld in the US Supreme Court, in preference to alternatives such as sharing the net benefit between producer and utility, or an average cost method which would embody prospects of an equity return for the utility.(1)

Thus the underlying philosophy for purchase tariffs embodied in the legislation of both countries, ie that of avoided cost, is virtually identical. It should be noted, though, that the policy of the esi in England and Wales moved to this principle in September 1979, almost four years before the 1983 Energy Act, following consideration of the Marshall report (2) into the potential for CHP in the UK. It had previously been based on the producer and the esi sharing the benefit. So given that the FERC rules were delayed by Court hearings the policy has been in place in both countries for a similar period of time.

4 PURCHASE TERMS IN THE UK

Because of the consultative process in England and Wales, the methods and principles agreed with the Government are uniformly applied in all of the 12 distributing Boards. The costs avoided by an Area Board purchasing privately generated electricity, and thus its worth to the producer, will be mainly the variable energy and capacity charges in the CEGB's bulk supply tariff. However, it will also depend upon the electrical relationship between the point on the system where the purchase is made, and the points on the system where the energy is subsequently sold by the Board. Broadly speaking it is found that the saved distribution losses of accepting an injection of private generation at a lower voltage than CEGB supplies are made available offsets the cost to the Board of absorbing and transporting the privately generated electricity to the point of use.

Whilst an injection of privately supplied electricity with a lower distribution voltage will lead to a corresponding reduction in the power flow from the CEGB through higher voltage distribution assets, the Board has a statutory duty to maintain supplies which is not shared by the private producer. It is therefore necessary to maintain or provide distribution capacity at the higher distribution voltages to standby to the possible failure or closure of the private generator's plant. Thus generally the capital costs of the distribution system are not avoided as the result of a private purchase.

The avoided costs of an Area Board in making a private purchase are usually those kW and kWh charges in the BST that vary with the quantity of power taken from the CEGB. The BST is, in accordance with Government advice (3), formulated to reflect the long run marginal costs of supply on the basis of an opportunity cost of capital for new investment of 5% pa in real terms. The kWh rates are determined from the incremental running costs of public supply generators needed to meet additional demand and vary both seasonally and with time of day. At times of high winter demand they are partly based on the running costs of oil plant but for the majority of the year they reflect the costs of coal plant which will be part loaded at night.

The capacity charge in the BST, and hence the capacity credit in the purchase tariff, reflects the cost of meeting increments of demand over the next 30 years (the average life of CEGB generating plant). In the early years of this period, whilst the CEGB has excess capacity, increments of demand can be met by retaining existing old plant on the system. However, as the surplus is eroded, it will be necessary eventually to build new plant to meet demand and the theory indicates (4) that the incremental cost of capacity will then rise to the cost of a gas turbine; this being the cheapest method of providing capacity for peak demand. To give the 'correct' pricing message the capacity charge in the BST is set at the levelised value of this rising staircase of annual capacity costs. Consequently the capacity credit in the purchase tariff, for a private generator that gives a continuous supply to the Area Board during weekday day hours in November to February, which is the period over which the CEGB's capacity charges apply, will total £31/kW in 1985/86; ie equal to the capacity charges in the BST. The capacity credit is given as a pence/kWh supplement thus ensuring that intermittent supplies receive a proportionately lower sum commensurate with their probability of avoiding the capacity costs of the Board purchasing the privately generated electricity.

Thus the purchase tariff reflects the long run marginal costs of electricity supply. At the present time of surplus capacity this will be above the cost which is avoided by the CEGB in the year of account but below the LRMC of a fully optimised system. For application to the private supplier the complex kWh rate schedule in the BST is simplified so that three rate metering can be used. In 1985/1986 with the CEGB's fossil fuel price at £52/te, the level is as follows:-

kWh prices paid to private generators between the hours (clocktime)	p/kWh
0030–0730	1.63
0730–0030 Sat and Sun 2000–0030 Mon – Fri 0730–2000 Mon – Fri, Mar–Oct	2.75
0730–2000 Mon-Fri, Nov & Feb	4.21
0730–2000 Mon-Fri, Dec & Jan	7.42

Where half hour recording metering is installed an additional payment of 2.48p/kWh during the 1½ hours of daily peak occuring on all days in October to May, and at weekends in June to September as retrospectively notified by the CEGB can be given under special terms. Where the point of injection of privately generated electricity is significantly better or worse in relation to the Board's load than that anticipated, this standard tariff could be modified for the changed cost situation with an increased or reduced offer made under special terms.

5 PURCHASE TERMS IN THE US

Although the FERC determined the basic guidelines for the principles on which US purchase terms must be based, section 210 of PURPA places the responsibility for implementing the FERC rules on the State public utility commission (PUC) which is the legal regulatory agency. In practice the FERC guidelines left considerable latitude to States and utilities in their interpretation of the rules and consequently there is wide variation in the purchase tariff methodologies that have been adopted although all will be based on avoided cost. In some instances PUCs have adopted a positive stance in devising the relevant guidelines, whilst in other States the utilities have been given the initial task of devising an appropriate methodology.

The most common methodology prescribed by state commissions for determining avoided energy costs is to estimate the heat rate associated with an increment of system load and multiply this figure by the cost of the marginal fuel. This approach closely follows the determination of the kWh rates in the CEGB's bulk supply tariff (BST) which are the basis for purchase tariffs in England and Wales. However, differences have emerged in defining the appropriate fuel cost to employ. In California the PUC originally decided that low sulphur oil was the relevant fuel but that the costs used should be those estimated for the coming quarter. Connecticut also identified oil as the incremental fuel, but required that the average cost the previous 12 months be employed. Consequently the energy credit is lower in Connecticut than in California.

For simplicity other commissions have looked to the running costs of a specific power station to detemine the avoided costs of the utility. Another approach that has been adopted to make the purchase rate readily identifiable is to use the same rate for power purchased from a "pool" arrangement as a proxy. Thus the utility would have to pay the same rate to a private producer as to a neighbouring utility.

As a number of commentators have pointed out, pool rates do not always reflect underlying marginal costs of the supplying authority which may be masked by other transactions in the pool arrangements.

The FERC rules give wider discretion in the payment of a credit for capacity since this is only required if the utility has a need for capacity. A number of PUCs have pronounced that their utilities do not have excess capacity and thus have not developed a methodology for determining the credit, whereas others have left the appropriate level for capacity to be individually negotiated between the utility and cogenerator. The most commonly adopted approach, though, is to link the credit for capacity to a specific plant type, usually a gas turbine, since this is the most frequently used method of meeting peak demands. This will directly mirror the situation in England and Wales when the CEGB system eventually achieves an optimal plant mix. Other methods proposed in the US include using the cost of capacity purchased from a 'pool' arrangement or another utility as a proxy, or determining the difference in capital cost between a utility's optimal capacity expansion plans with and without the QF.

The differences in the methodologies adopted by State PUCs, and the wide range of underlying energy and capacity costs has led to considerable variability in the level of payment individual utilities will make for purchases from QFs up to 100kW. A 1982 US Department of Energy Survey (5) found that standard purchase rates varied from 1.0 cents/kWh in Nebraska to 8.0 cents/kWh in Vermont. Eleven states, mostly in the Midwest, were found to offer rates of 2.0 cents/kWh or less, whereas 14 states had rates greater than 5.0 cents/kWh. Thirteen of these fourteen states were found to be heavily dependant on oil for meeting incremental demand and the survey notes that these rates would fluctuate with oil prices, or fall abruptly when the last oil-fired plant was retired from the utility's system. Overall, purchase rates average 3.77 cents/kWh across the US which compares with an average payment in the UK in 1984/85 of 4.0 cents/kWh (2.7p/kWh) for a continuously operating generator.

PURPA section 210 requires that PUCs establish standard purchase rates for QFs up to 100kW capacity. However, for larger supplies some States require standard contracts to be offered with others expecting terms to be individually negotiated. PUC involvement in negotiated contracts also varies between States with some requiring only that contracts be filed, but others specifying Commission approval of the contracts. 70% of PUCs will arbitrate between utility and private generator in devising the terms. A survey by the Edison Electric Institute in 1983 (6) indicates that of 47 States.

17 required standard contracts for QFs up to 10MW
7 specified short term standard contracts (1-5 years) and
5 specified long term standard contracts (5-30 years).

Where contracts were negotiated

4 states required these to be long term
17 required only filing of the contracts, but
15 sought PUC approval, and
32 States provide for the Commission to arbitrate.

6   CALIFORNIAN PURCHASE ARRANGEMENTS

Purchase tariffs in California are often quoted (7) when comparing the impact of the US and UK legislation, and the Californian Public Utilities Commission has played a leading role (8) in developing the avoided cost concept promulgated by FERC.

In the US Dept. of Energy survey the purchase rates for Californian QFs under 100kW averaged 6.5 cents/kWh reflecting the fact that all Californian utilities originally determined avoided energy costs from oil, although most fossil fuelled generating plant can be dual fired by either gas or oil. The fuel position has been somewhat distorted by the regulation of gas prices which have been held at an artificially high level for electricity generation. However, a fall in underlying gas prices has resulted in gas becoming the marginal fuel from August 1985 with a consequent reduction in the energy rate of 1¢/kWh. Marginal costs have also been reduced by the recent commissioning of two nuclear stations.

The majority of State PUCs expect payments for capacity to be derived from costs avoided in the year of account but 8 States take a more generous stance towards the private generator and either required or encouraged, as in the case of California, the purchase rates to be levelised over the life of the contracted output. Of course this will usually be a shorter period than the 30 year levelisation undertaken in determining the capacity credit in England and Wales. In California, where a situation of capacity shortage existed at the time PURPA was enacted, the cost of a gas turbine is used to determine the level of the capacity payment since this is the cheapest type of plant for meeting peak demand. Similarly, when the surplus capacity in England and Wales is eventually absorbed, and the plant mix optimised, the capacity credit in Area Board purchase tariffs will also revert to the capital costs of the gas turbine. Purchase tariff rates are thus higher in California than in England and Wales because utility marginal fuel costs were previously oil and are now regulated gas instead of predominantly coal, and a situation of surplus capacity does not exist.

Californian purchase arrangements following PURPA have been structured around four standard offers which may be summarised as follows:-

Offer 1 is intended for intermittent supplies from renewable sources that export to the public system at the discretion of the QF. Payment for energy is based on the running costs of marginal oil plant and is separately calculated for seasonal and daily load variations. The avoided capacity cost is determined from the cost of gas turbine plant that would have been installed but for the purchase. This sum is adjusted for the reliability of the producer, allocated to peak periods and expressed as a kWh supplement.

Offer 2 is devised for cogeneration plant that has firm capacity that can be contracted at the same reliability as utility plant. Energy payments are determined as for offer 1. Similarly capacity payments, now expressed as $/kW, are determined from the cost of gas turbine plant but over the duration of the contract and levelised, with no correction for reliability.

Offer 3 is the standard offer required under s.210 of PURPA for QF's up to 100kW. Rates are determined as in offer 1 but an average correction for reliability is made so that the terms can be applied irrespective of the QF's technology.

Offer 4 had the purpose of reducing the financing problems and commercial risks to a QF by deriving energy rates from forecasts of energy costs over the duration of the contract period (in excess of 15 years). The QF had the choice of being paid actual energy rates determined as for offer 1, forecast energy costs for the early part of the contract period, or a levelised energy payment rate over the duration of the contract. Payments for capacity would be as in offer 1 for intermittent supplies or as in offer 2 for firm supplies.

With expectations in the period 1980-1983 of oil prices increasing in real terms the levelised values under offer 4 will have been significantly greater than the published rates calculated for offers 1-3. As a consequence it is understood that virtually all QFs have obtained contracts under offer 4. Since the electricity revenues are defined and virtually guaranteed for the life of the plant, offer 4 has had considerable appeal for prospective financiers of schemes. Generally this has made it possible for promoters to consider funding schemes mainly with loan finance.

The 11GW of private generation in California, of which a little over 40% is cogeneration, that is either commissioned or for which there are signed contracts accounts for a large proportion of the capacity needed by the system up until the mid nineties. In addition the recent commissioning of new nuclear stations has also added to available capacity and reduced incremental costs. As a consequence the PUC decided to suspend offer 4 from April 1985. It remains to be seen whether new schemes continue to emerge at the same rate now that 'front end' loading of electricity credits are no longer available. Payment in advance of anticipated real terms increases in energy costs would not be a prospect in the UK since it must result in consumers paying more for their electricity in the short run which would be contrary to s.7 of the Energy Act. Similarly, it is probably not possible for Area Boards to conclude long term contracts with defined capacity payments since if these were lower than the cost actually avoided through the bulk supply tariff then the Board would be obliged to increase the payment accordingly, or if the contracted payment was above that actually avoided by the Board it would result in consumers paying more for their electricity.

7   AVERAGE AND MARGINAL COSTS

Although the FERC guidelines impose marginal cost principles on purchase arrangements most US utilities still employ average cost pricing as their basis for industrial and domestic supply tariffs. This can lead to a number of anomolous situations which might favour the emergence of privately operated cogeneration in some States. Figure 1 demonstrates that at times of plant shortage average costs will lie below marginal costs. Utilities in this situation which price at average cost will make it more attractive for investment to be undertaken by QFs than by themselves. This position would be aggrevated if PUCs as the result of political pressure for price restraint, hold down the level of price utilities can charge. This can be a frequent phenomenon with PUCs reluctant to allow price increases unless additional accounting costs, resulting perhaps from the construction of new power stations, can be demonstrated. In the UK the present position of surplus plant results in marginal costs being less than average costs, but since both purchase and supply tariffs are formulated on marginal cost principles both electricity supply and demand are subject to the same pricing messages.

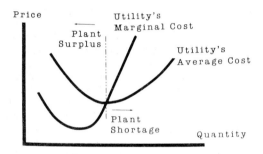

Fig 1   Utility's average and marginal costs

The juxtaposition of marginally costed purchase tariffs and average costed supply tariffs, sometimes restrained by the regulatory process, has resulted in a number of situations where QFs could purchase electricity from their host utility at a lower price than could be gained for their own generation. The 1982 US Dept. of Energy survey noted that in eight States, including California, the purchase rates exceeded the typical industrial rate. The situation is thrown into sharper relief by contracted arrangements where the utility purchases the entire output of a private generator's plant and separately supplies the private generator's load. This has enabled the private producer to conduct an arbitrage operation in supplying and consuming electricity. Rather than abandon the basis for the purchase tariff Californian PUC staff are currently seeking the application of marginal cost principles to supply tariffs also (9) to overcome this situation.

8   US COGENERATION

Interest in the prospects for industrial CHP is promoted generally by the high cost of energy which argues for conservation in use. However, the quantity of CHP likely to emerge can be predicted from a micro economic model developed by Joskow and Jones (10). This demonstrates that the quantity of industrial CHP is likely to vary inversely with the incremental cost of fuel over and above that used to produce heat from heat only boilers, but directly with the value of the electricity produced. The value of electricity produced will either be the cost of the electricity previously purchased from the utility if the CHP electrical output is consumed entirely on the cogenerator's site, or the purchase tariff if the output is sold to the utility. In the former case this will be related to either the average or marginal fuel cost of the utility depending upon the electricity pricing methodology that has been adopted, and in the latter case to the avoided (ie marginal) cost. Furthermore cogenerated power is likely to vary inversely with the incremental costs of providing CHP capacity, as opposed to heat only boilers, and directly with the steam load factor.

Early forecasts following the enactment of PURPA suggested that the major steam using industrial sectors of pulp and paper, chemicals and petroleum refining, which account for the majority of the industrial steam load, would show a bullish response to the legislation. It was predicted (11) that their total cogeneration capacity would more than double between 1980 and 1990. The impact of PURPA can now be examined from the FERC filings of qualifying facilities. The situation at the end of 1983 has been published (12) and lists 204 cogenerators representing new capacity of 6.4GW. Over 40% of these filings were for plants in California, with Florida and Texas accounting for a further 15%. In terms of capacity Texas contributed almost 40% of the rated capacity, and California, Florida and Massachusettes a further 40%. In the other 46 states PURPA legislation appears to have had minimal impact. The main impetus for cogeneration in these states is probably attributable to avoided costs being based on oil or natural gas. California, Florida and Massachusettes all have purchase rates in excess of 5¢/kWh exclusive of any capacity credit. It has also been noted (13) that the major utilities in these four states all offer 'simultaneous sale and purchase arrangements' which allows the private generator the prospect of conducting an arbitrage operation. Favourable tax benefits have also been suggested as an added stimulus to investment.

However, filing as a QF with FERC does not necessarily mean that the proposed CHP plant will be constructed. A recent study by the National Economic Research Association (14) indicates that by August 1984 a total of 11.8GW of cogeneration was operational representing around 2% of all US generation. This compares with a proportion of possibly 4% in Great Britain. Around one half of CHP plant is located in the South Atlantic and West South Central regions of the US. Of the individual states Texas has the most cogeneration with over 3.6GW installed; mainly in the petrochemical industry. California is a distant second with 0.75MW commissioned which is only a fraction of the 4GW noted above that is filed with FERC.

9   CONCLUSIONS

This review has demonstrated the close similarity between PURPA and the 1983 Energy Act both in its intent, ie, to increase competition, and in its requirement that the terms offered for the purchase of electricity from a cogenerator, or other private producer, should be based on the avoided costs of the utility. However, whereas the avoided costs in England and Wales are predominantly those of coal plant, in the United States they can vary widely from a low level reflecting a significant proportion of hydro plant to a relatively high figure where the utility's marginal plant is oil fired. Similarly the credit given for capacity by US utilities can vary from zero, where there is a surplus of capacity, to a figure based on the annualised cost of a gas turbine. In England and Wales where surplus capacity also exists the capacity cost message is derived by levelising the future costs of capacity over a 30 year time horizon. Only a few States adopt this approach, and where this is the practice the time scale chosen is the contract duration indicating that the methodology in England and Wales is intrinsically more generous although costs are lower.

Both supply and purchase tariffs in the UK are derived from long run marginal cost principles, but this is not generally the case in the US where most utilities continue to use average costs for determining supply tariffs. This can lead to an anomolous situation in some cases with the purchase tariff set at a higher level than the normal industrial supply tariff. Under these circumstances the private producer will prefer to sell his output to the utility rather than displace the public supply for his own consumption and there is an abnormal incentive for investment.

A further stimulus in the US to investment by the cogenerator in preference to the utility has been the practice in a few States of basing the avoided energy costs on future anticipated oil prices. These forecasts have proved to be substantially overstated and recently the approach has been suspended in California. With a less pessimistic view on future movements in oil prices, and a downward revision in electricity demand forecasts, projections of the likely potential for cogeneration may well be reduced accordingly.

In the UK lower electricity prices and incremental costs of electricity production than in some US utilities, and other factors such as declining heat/power ratios in industry, make investment in combined heat and power less favourable. In addition, the effective requirement of the Energy Act that the private producer should shoulder the risk associated with a forecast of fuel price movements has mitigated against any significant upturn in industrial cogeneration. Whilst it is perhaps still too early to comment on the effectiveness of the Act in stimulating private production of electricity it must also be noted that the Act did not produce a step change in policy since, unlike the situation in the US prior to PURPA, the esi in England and Wales had already adopted a policy of basing its purchase arrangements on avoided cost.

REFERENCES

(1)   GUNN, E.M. BALLARD, S.C. DEVINE, M.D PURPA: Issues in Federal and State Implementation, Policy Studies Journal, US (2) December 1984.

(2)   Energy Paper 35, Combined Heat and Electrical Power Generation in the UK, 1979, HMSO.

(3)   Cmnd 7131, The Nationalised Industries, 1977, HMSO.

(4)   TURVEY, R. Optimal Pricing and Investment in Electricity Supply. 1968, Allen & Unwin, London.

(5)   US Energy Information Administration, Cogeneration: Regulation, Economics and Capacity, 1983, Vol 1, p. 49 et seq.

(6)   GUNN, E.M et al, Op Cit, p. 358.

(7)   Third report from the Select Committee on Energy Session 1982-83, Vol 1, para 59, April 1983, HMSO.

(8)   CALIFORNIA PUC, Handbook of Cogeneration Pricing Methodologies, 1981, US Department of Energy.

(9)   CALIFORNIA PUC, Talking Points and Figures, March 1985, Staff Paper.

(10) JOSKOW, P.L. Industrial Cogeneration and Electricity Production in the US, Jan 1982, Discussion paper for US Dept of Energy.

(11) DE RENZO, D.J. Cogeneration Technology and Economics for the Process Industries, 1983, Noyes Data Corporation, New Jersey, USA.

(12) WOOSTER, C. THOMPSON, E. PAYNE, F. How well are PURPA's Cogeneration Incentives Functioning, Cogeneration Sourcebook Ch. 11, 1985.

(13) WOOSTER, C. et al, Op Cit, p. 169.

(14) Cogeneration: Can utilities make it pay, Electrical World, December 1985.

Two co-generation plants in California, USA

H L HARKINS, BSEE, PE, MASME, MIEEE, MPES, MIAS
Hawker Siddeley Power Engineering, Inc.

SYNOPSIS   This paper describes the general economic and technical environment in which were developed two similar cogeneration plants addressing the need for power and refrigeration load at two cold storage facilities in the vicinity of Los Angeles. Each plant comprises a single LM-2500 gas turbine with a dual pressure waste heat boiler generating steam to both an extraction-condensing steam turbine-generator and an absorption refrigeration unit. Included is a description of the cycle together with the factors leading to the choice of the alternative method of financing the projects. Both plants are situated on congested sites in a developed area and consideration of environmental factors is described. The operational characteristics together with the operating regime and staff is considered.

1   PROJECT DEVELOPMENT

The projects described herein were developed as third party owned facilities, namely neither the electric utility nor the thermal users provided capital or debt for the construction of the facilities. The development originated with Sunlaw Energy Corporation, a California firm founded by Mr. Robert N. Danziger, for the express purpose of developing cogeneration projects.

The ownership of the projects is within a Partnership consisting of the general partners and a number of limited partners. Sunlaw will manage the projects pursuant to a management agreement for terms up to 25 years.

2   CONSTRUCTING, OWNING AND OPERATING COGENERATION POWER PLANTS

Constructing, owning and operating cogeneration facilities like these described herein includes (1) leasing or purchasing the facility site; (2) designing and constructing the facility; (3) maintaining the facility by repairing or replacing worn-out, damaged or defective parts; (4) monitoring energy production; (5) assuring a supply of fuel for the facility; (6) selling the electricity generated by the facility to a utility or other energy user; (7) selling the thermal energy generated by the facility for industrial processes or for commercial heating or cooling purposes; and (8) continuously reviewing the regulatory environment to ensure that the facility complies at all times with all applicable regulations.

3   DESCRIPTION OF THE COGENERATION FACILITIES

Sunlaw entered into two turnkey, fixed price Construction Agreements with Hawker Siddeley Power Engineering Inc of Houston, Texas to provide overall management and coordination of the design, engineering, construction and startup activities associated with each project. Hawker Siddeley Power Engineering Inc is a wholly-owned subsidiary of H S Investments Inc., which in turn is a wholly-owned subsidiary of Hawker Siddeley Group Public Limited Company.

The two facilities described herein are substantially identical. The major power generation component in each plant is a Model LM-2500 gas turbine engine as manufactured by General Electric Co. The LM-2500 is generally regarded as one of the most efficient gas turbine engines produced today. An aircraft-derivative engine used commonly in the Boeing 747 and other jumbo jets, the LM-2500 was designed to operate under the stringent reliability and performance criteria required by the aviation industry. Historical operating data maintained by General Electric indicate that the availability factor of the LM-2500 typically exceeds 99 percent in aviation usage.

The LM-2500 was packaged along with a Brush electric generator, air filtration and generator cooling systems, and associated auxiliary equipment (such as lube oil pumps) into a single, skid-mounted steel housing by Stewart & Stevenson of Houston, Texas. In the unit package the LM-2500 drives the Brush generator providing an approximate site-rated power output of 21.3 megawatts.

The gas turbine discharges high temperature (approximately 960° Farenheit) exhaust heat into a heat recovery boiler to generate approximately 71,000 pounds per hour of intermediate pressure, superheated steam (600 pounds per square inch at 700° Farenheit) and 6900 lbs/hr of low pressure saturated steam (120 psig at 350° Farenheit). The heat recovery boiler for each plant was supplied by Henry Vogt Machine Company of Louisville, Kentucky.

The 600 psig steam is delivered to an extraction steam turbine which drives a second Brush induction generator providing additional electric power output. On the average, the steam turbine generator will provide a power output of approximately 5.5 megawatts resulting in a total, average system electrical output capacity of approximately 26.8 megawatts from each plant. The steam turbine for each plant was provided by Coppus-Murray, a subsidiary of Coppus Engineering Corporation.

The Coppus-Murray extraction steam turbine is designed to enable a variable amount of reduced pressure steam (120 psig) to be extracted from the mid-point of the turbine. The amount of extraction steam flow will vary in proportion to increases or decreases in the refrigeration customer's cooling load. Steam not needed for extraction to meet the cooling loads is expanded through the remaining sections of the steam turbine to drive the generator, thereby providing additional electric power output from the plant. This steam is ultimately condensed in a surface condenser, and the liquid condensate is returned in a closed cycle to the heat recovery boiler. Cooling water for the condenser is supplied from an on-site three-cell cooling tower provided by the Marley Co.

The 120 psig steam from the Vogt heat recovery boiler and additional 120 psig steam from the Coppus-Murray extraction steam turbine will be reduced to 110 psig for use in the ammonia absorption refrigeration process unit of each plant. The refrigeration systems were designed by Borsig GmbH, a West German corporation whose refrigeration systems are presently utilized in more than 125 installations in 25 countries.

The plants' ammonia absorption refrigeration equipment chills ammonia to -50° Farenheit. This chilled ammonia is delivered within a closed system to a heat exchanger to which the closed ammonia systems at the cold storage facilities are connected, thereby cooling the ammonia on the users' side of the heat exchanger to -40° Farenheit. The ammonia in the plants is not commingled at any point with the ammonia of the cold storage systems. Feedback of operating disturbances between the two systems will therefore be minimized.

Each plant is designed to operate 24 hours a day, seven days a week. After allowing for scheduled and unscheduled downtime for inspection, maintenance and repairs, the expected long term availability of each plant will be 95 percent (8322 hours per year), resulting in an annual electrical energy production of approximately 223 million kilowatt hours.

The ammonia absorption refrigeration systems of the two plants are not identical because of slightly different refrigeration loads and temperature requirements at the cold storage warehouses. The refrigeration system is capable of delivering up to 1000 tons of refrigeration in the form of chilled ammonia at -50° Fahrenheit in the case of one of the plants and 900 tons in the case of the other plant, resulting in an annual thermal energy production capacity (assuming 95 percent availability) of 8.3 million and 7.5 million ton-hours of refrigeration per year, respectively.

Fuel use requirements for firing each LM-2500 is approximately constant, regardless of the extraction steam flow rate. The LM-2500 has been designed to require approximately 10 900 Btu of energy to produce one kilowatt hour of electricity (i.e., a "heat rate" of 10 900 Btu/Kwh) under site-rated conditions. On the average, the steam generated by the heat recovery boiler provides an additional 5.5 megawatts of electricity without any additional fuel use, thereby improving the plants' efficiency and reducing their expected average heat rate to 8550 Btu/Kwh. Allowing for an average 1.5 percent degradation in performance results in an annual average heat rate of 8678 Btu/Kwh. To produce its average total output capacity of 26.8 megawatts, each plant requires approximately 232.6 million Btu of fuel per hour. Based on 95 percent availability, the total annual fuel use requirement of each plant is approximately 1.94 million MBtu, or approximately 1.9 billion cubic feet of natural gas. Natural gas is supplied to each LM-2500 through a dedicated intertie to a high pressure main. If necessary, the fuel is further compressed on-site to system pressure. Power output from the generators is fed into the utility grid at 66 kilovolts through switchgear and transformers located on-site.

A number of additional features are expected to enhance the reliability of the plants. The LM-2500 is incorporated into a special modular system design which permits the builder to warrant a maximum 48-hour turnaround time for maintenance. In the event of a temporary curtailment in natural gas supply, the LM-2500 can switch immediately to fuel oil with no disruption in service. Enough fuel oil to permit continuous operation for at least 20 hours will be permanently stored on each plant site, and the owner has obtained environmental permits which will allow operation of each plant on No. 2 fuel oil for up to approximately 52 days per year. Finally, each plant is designed to maintain its electrical power generating capacity unimpaired even when the refrigeration unit is completely out of service: design capacity of the cooling tower and surface condenser is sufficient to condense all 71 000 lbs/hr of high pressure steam expanded through the turbine.

A Fisher PROVOX distributed control system (DCS) is employed in the system design for centralized control allowing a system management with minimal attending operators as well as continuous event data recording. The DCS also interfaces with a programmable controller for the water treatment system and motors throughout the plant to provide the operator with a single window for control.

4 SOURCES OF FUNDS AND PROJECT COSTS

The following summarizes the sources of funds and project costs during the construction period:

Sources of Funds
(US $000)

Equity..................................	$21 717
Term Debt..............................	48 800
Total Sources.........................	$70 517

Project Costs
(US $000)

Fixed Price Costs, Interest during Construction, Sales Taxes, Refrigeration Interties, Spare Parts, and Equipment Contingency...............	61 200
Construction Management Fees and Expense Reimbursement, Insurance, Site Lease Payments, Financial Fees, Working Capital, Legal, Accounting, Printing, etc..............	6 284
Debt and Equity Placement and Financial Advisory, Investor Services, and Partnership Administration Fees...................	3 033
Total Project Costs..............	$70 517

5 ECONOMIC FACTORS

The two plants produce electricity for sale to the utility under a contract with a minimum term of 20 years, and refrigeration for sale to the cold storage facilities under renewable 15-year contracts. The sale of electricity to the utility is expected to provide 98 percent of the operating revenue, and the sale of thermal energy is expected to provide the other two percent.

The plants represent income-producing assets not subject to the normal risks of uncertain demands, market overcapacity or competition. The economic success of the plants depends on their efficiency and availability and on future energy prices. Each of the following events will increase the projects' cash flow assuming that all other factors remain constant:

o   Utility fuel prices are either less than or more than $30 per barrel of low sulphur crude oil;

o   Rates for natural gas charged to industrial users in the area fall below rates charged to utility users;

o   The utility uses fuel oil that is more expensive than the industrial price for natural gas;

o   The utility generating facilities degrade in performance; and

o   Cogeneration plant performance exceeds assumptions.

The power sales agreement requires the utility to pay for all electricity produced by the cogeneration plants. The utility's purchase price will be based on a formula which reflects their average cost of generating electricity in its oil- and gas-fired plants, but the utility will in no event pay the project less than 5.8 cents/Kwh. Given the expected efficiency of the utilities oil- and gas-fired power plants, the formula price and the minimum price will be equal when the utilities cost of fuel is approximately $30 per barrel of low sulphur crude oil (or approximately $5.16 per million Btu for natural gas). If the utilities fuel costs exceed this level, the price they will pay for electricity generation in the cogeneration plants will increase. However, if fuel costs are less than this level, the project will continue to receive payment based on the floor price. The utility will also pay for the approximately 54 megawatts of capacity the plants will supply to the grid on a basis unrelated to future energy prices.

Fuel prices will determine a major component of the revenues from the utility as well as its principal expense. In the event that fuel prices are less than the $30 per barrel level, however, electrical energy payments from the utility will remain at the floor price while the projects fuel expense will decrease. Accordingly, project cash flow should increase. For each $1 per million Btu decrease in fuel prices below such level, that cash available to the project for the payment of non-fuel expenses, reserves and distributions will increase by approximately $667 000 per annum (assuming all other expenses remain constant).

If fuel prices increase above the floor price level, the project cash flow will also increase because the plants are expected to operate more efficiently than the utilities oil- and gas-fired facilities.

As a result of the design of the plants, it is expected that they will consume, on the average, approximately 25 percent less fuel than the utility oil- and gas-fired plants to generate the same quantity of electrical energy. Consequently, an increase in the price of fuel will increase the average cost of generating electricity in the utility oil- and gas-fired plants more than in the cogeneration plants (assuming that the price paid by the project for fuel does not increase more than the price paid by the utility).

Consequently, since the price paid by the utility to the project will be based on the average cost of generating electricity in the utility oil- and gas-fired plants, rising fuel prices will increase the utilities payments to the project more than the projects' fuel expense will increase. For each $1 per million Btu increase in energy prices above the floor price level, the cash available to the project for the payment of non-fuel expenses, reserves and distributions will increase by approximately $217 000 per annum (assuming all other expenses remain constant). Moreover, as the utility plants continue to degrade due to equipment aging or operation at part load efficiencies, the increased relative efficiency of the cogeneration plants will produce additional cash flow for the project.

6 CASH FLOW FORECAST AND SENSITIVITY

The significant factors affecting cash flow are:

o unit fuel difference per kilowatt-hour between the utility and the cogeneration plant;

o fuel unit price difference paid by the utility and by the cogenerator;

o future fuel prices;

o available operating hours per year; and

o interest rates during construction and at refinancing of construction debt.

Cash flow is provided by the excess of revenues from operations over operating expenses and debt services. The principal components of cash flow can be divided into (1) electric energy and refrigeration revenues and fuel expense, which are related to energy prices, (2) capacity revenues and debt service which are related to the total capacity of the plants, and (3) non-fuel expenses which are based on neither (1) nor (2) above.

Net energy revenues will be determined principally by (1) the difference in the amount of, or price for, fuel required by the utility and the cogeneration plants to produce each kilowatt-hour of electricity, (2) future energy prices, and (3) cogeneration plant availability. Net capacity revenues will principally be determined by (1) cogeneration plant availability and (2) interest rates during construction of the plants and at refinancing of the Construction/Term Loan.

7 OPERATIONS

Sunlaw and Stewart & Stevenson have executed an Operations and Maintenance Agreement under which Stewart & Stevenson will provide operations and maintenance services for the plants. The Agreement will have a three-year term beginning with the completion of the first plant, renewable for up to four additional three-year terms. Stewart & Stevenson will provide personnel to operate the plants, service plant equipment, and carry out scheduled preventive maintenance and inspections.

Labor requirements are estimated according to the following schedule:

1 Plant Superintendent
1 Operations Manager
9 Stationary Operators
2 Technicians
1 Mechanic
2 Utility Men

Total annual salary costs for the required staff is estimated at less than $500 000. In addition, an amount will be allocated to personnel insurance and other benefits, administrative expenses such as office and payroll, and other overhead related costs, resulting in annual labor costs of approximately $900 000. Stewart & Stevenson estimates that total costs for management services, annual inspections, service, maintenance, spare parts replacement, and miscellaneous supplies will be approximately $300 000.

Based on the foregoing assumptions, total annual operations and maintenance expenses are forecast to be $1 200 000 in 1984 dollars. It is assumed that operations and maintenance expenses will escalate at six percent per annum from the original estimates until commencement of operations in 1986, continuing to escalate at six percent per annum thereafter.

8 LOCAL FACTORS

A key criterion in the development of power generating facilities in the locale selected is obtaining necessary permits for emissions which are controlled by local, state, and federal authorities.

Among the several emissions from the plants the control of nitrous oxides (NO_x) is one of the most critical. While federal authority limits allow 75 ppm the local limit for which the plants were permitted is approximately 60 ppm. This limit is obtained by water injection into the gas turbine combustion area utilizing boiler condensate as the water source.

9 CONCLUSION

The Sunlaw development represents a major step in the development of an emerging non-regulated power generation industry via the techniques and principles of cogeneration.

The significant financing mechanism used for development of the project (i.e., a third party owned facility without using the host site's credit or balance sheet resources) opens the door to the development of subsequent facilities at virtually any site irrespective of the host site's own financial capabilities.

The net result is a more efficiently produced commodity (i.e. electrical and thermal energy), at locations generally at the point of usage, developed through private financings at lower cost per kilowatt than conventional generating schemes.

10 ACKNOWLEDGEMENTS

The author is indebted to the assistance provided by Sunlaw principals and their consultants and associates in providing much of the background data and permission for use of the information presented herein.